Praise for Levonne Louie's
Mineral Land Rights: What You Need to Know:

"Ms. Louie has managed to explain the concept of ownership of mineral rights in layman's terms. This is a useful book for land-owners and industry members alike." **DAVID YOUNGGREN,** QC, *lawyer and landowner*

"This book is practical, balanced, and timely. It makes a complicated topic manageable." **ROSS HARVEY,** *agri-marketer, founding partner of AdFarm, and landowner*

"Ms. Louie has written the definitive guide for landowners. Readers will find themselves repeatedly referring back to Chapter 8 until it is dog-eared." **JUDITH ATHAIDE,** *P.Eng.,* MBA

"*Mineral Land Rights* is as useful to the layman as it is to newcomers to the energy business." **BRIAN SKINNER,** *P.Geol., geologist*

"Get informed quickly with this plain-language guide to mineral land. *Mineral Land Rights* provides a wealth of information, and Levonne Louie's thirty-five-plus years of land experience place her in a unique position to deliver all fundamental concepts of mineral land in an intelligent yet concise and easy-to-read format." **JOAN DORNIAN,** *oil and gas lawyer*

"*Mineral Land Rights* is straightforward, is written in easily understood language, and presents the material in logical progressive building blocks. It would be of interest to both surface and mineral freehold landowners as well as to oil and gas industry personnel. It's well written and can be easily digested, whether or not you have a background in the field. **JONAS L. ALBECK,** R., *Retired Landman and Consul of Denmark, Emeritus*

"*Mineral Land Rights* is a must-read for those who want to understand the basics of mineral rights ownership. A starting point for those new to the concepts of title ownership and mineral leasing, the book also serves as a primer for those who may already be engaged in the industry without extensive experience in land ownership and administration. I highly recommend this resource as required reading for all students of land negotiations, land contracts, and lease administration." **JONATHAN CHAPMAN,** *B. Comm., P.Land, President, Legacy Land and Title Company Inc.*

"At a recent conference where I met with many landowners with mineral rights, I was amazed at the range of complaints, misunderstandings, and lack of knowledge they had about mineral rights. This book should be the bible for every landowner and mineral rights holder. It has become a welcome resource to even my most experienced land people." **DEBBIE DEGENSTEIN,** *President/Landman, Pinnacle Consulting Services Inc.*

"Levonne Louie has managed to capture the essence of what mineral land signifies, all in succinct prose that everyone can read and appreciate. I wish this book had been available twenty years ago." **FRANÇOIS MARÉCHAL,** *P.Geol. AB; P.Geol. BC; AAPG Canada Region President 2013-15; Exploration Geology Manager—New Ventures, Quicksilver Resources Canada Inc.*

"Accurate, informative, plain-language explanations of any regulatory field ought to be welcome contributions to any literature. Levonne Louie's new book certainly fits this bill." **FENNER STEWART,** *Assistant Professor of Law at the University of Calgary, in Resources: Canadian Institute of Resources Law*

UPSTREAM

UP

LEVONNE LOUIE

STREAM

OIL AND GAS EXPLORATION

AND PRODUCTION

AN OVERVIEW

Citrine PRESS

Citrine Press
Suite 2202, 1078 6th Avenue SW
Calgary AB
Canada T2P 5N6

Cataloguing data available from Library and Archives Canada
ISBN 978-0-9938037-2-7 (paperback)
ISBN 978-0-9938037-3-4 (ebook)

Publishing consulting by Jesse Finkelstein at Page Two Strategies
Editing by Lana Okerlund
Proofreading by Jennifer Stewart
Cover and text design by Peter Cocking

15 16 17 18 19   5 4 3 2 1

Contents

THIS BOOK IS not intended to provide legal or technical advice, as I am not a lawyer, engineer, or geologist. However, I have over thirty-six years of experience in the oil and gas industry that I would like to share. The information in this book will, I hope, provide a basic understanding of the oil and gas exploration process to allow those interested in the industry to develop a foundation from which they can ask questions and start to engage in conversations about the energy industry.

Acknowledgements

THE IDEA FOR writing this book came as I was working on my first book, *Mineral Land Rights: What You Need to Know* and crystallized following the release of that book. I found there are a lot of people, both inside and outside the oil and gas industry, who are interested in learning more about the industry and how oil and gas is found.

Within the industry, many people are caught in the silos of their professions. While they might be interested in learning about the other sectors in the industry and how those sectors affect their jobs, they might not be given the opportunity to expand their knowledge base within their positions. Outside the industry, there are many people interested in learning more about oil and gas, as discussions about energy are happening more often in their lives.

Other than attending expensive, time-consuming courses, there aren't many resource guides that explain the essential concepts of the oil and gas industry in easy-to-understand terms. I think I have accomplished this with this book but I wouldn't have been able to do so without the help of my team.

I would like to thank Jesse Finkelstein of Page Two Strategies for her support, patience, wisdom, creativity and guidance as she helped me through the process. She continues to demystify the strange, new world of publishing for me. Her assistance with the myriad details that I didn't even know about has been invaluable. In addition, bringing back together my team of professionals to work on this second book made the process relatively seamless and painless. Her professionalism added greatly to the final product.

Thank you also goes to my designer, Peter Cocking, for his patience and skill. The creativity he has applied to my books gives them a professional look that helps them stand out.

There are other members of my team who deserve a great deal of thanks. My copyeditor, Lana Okerlund, edited the words so that I could better express myself. Jen Stewart used her proofreading skills to make sure there were no "glitches" in the text. Kaleeg Hainsworth used his skills to convert the book to e-book format for those readers who prefer an e-book version. Thank you to all the members of my team for helping me to deliver a professional product.

Thank you to Brian Skinner who read the book and provided corrections and suggestions on the content. Your assistance is invaluable and I greatly appreciate your efforts.

Thank you to Randy White and Sean Fairhurst for reading my book and agreeing to provide endorsements. I greatly value your opinions and I am humbled by your comments.

I owe a great deal of thanks to all the oil and gas professionals I have met through the years and from whom I have learned so much. Their willingness to share their wisdom and their patience with all of my questions is greatly appreciated.

Finally, thank you to my daughter, Megan Mah, for your love and support. You continue to inspire me to be the best person I can be and you encourage me to follow my dreams, no matter where I am in my life's journey. I am proud to be your Mom.

Introduction

Why Have I Written This Book?

MY INTENTION IN writing this book is to put into layman's terms what is known as the upstream portion of
the oil and gas industry—that is, the exploration and production phase in which companies decide where they would
like to drill, acquire land, drill a well, apply the necessary
processes to the well so the oil or gas can be brought to the
surface (known as completing the well), produce the product,
gather it, and then take it to a sales point where they can sell
it to someone. This is the part of the industry that deals with
finding oil and gas and includes everything that happens
before it gets to a refinery to be processed into the products
that you and I use on an everyday basis.

In my first book, *Mineral Land Rights: What You Need to
Know,* I provided a basic overview to the oil and gas industry, including how various companies in the industry might

be described. In addition, I focused on a necessary, early step in the process: identifying and securing mineral rights. Whereas the first book concentrated on this one key element, this book expands its focus and explores the many steps in the exploration process.

While the land principles described in my first book focused on western Canada, the information provided in this book focuses on the process of exploration and the upstream side of the oil and gas industry. The basic components of this exploration and production process can be applied to many different parts of the world. Some parts of the process may get or need more attention than other areas depending on, for example, whether the well being drilled is an exploration well or a development well. More science might be conducted on an exploration well to confirm that the target formation has been reached, whereas this may be unnecessary on a development well for which lots of information is available from nearby wells. Another example is when a company is drilling in a remote area with extreme weather conditions compared to an easily accessible area with more moderate weather. Different equipment may be required to operate under harsh conditions, and the logistics of preparing to drill a well can be much more time-consuming. Similarly, special equipment will be necessary when drilling offshore compared to onshore, or when a large volume of hydrocarbons under high formation pressures is expected from a well compared to small volumes of hydrocarbons under low pressures.

Some companies may emphasize one part of the process more than other companies. For example, a major integrated company may want to apply more tests for research purposes than a small independent junior company would want to do. The rigour applied to different stages of the process may depend on the size of the company and its tolerance for risk. However, when it comes right down to it, the processes are similar.

This book does not address the special processes used in the part of the Alberta oilsands that require mining techniques that are very different from more conventional drilling methods. Other resources are available for mining operations.

There tends to be some mystique around the oil and gas industry due to the numerous technical issues involved in the process and the many technical terms that are used. In this book, I attempt to describe those processes in non-technical terms so the average person on the street will understand them. My hope is that if more people understand the processes involved, there will be a better understanding of the oil and gas industry in general—which in turn will lead to better dialogue between various groups as we address currently evolving issues and those that will present themselves in the future. For example, if you understand the what, how, and why of the processes that go into completing a well, you may be more comfortable discussing the pros and cons of one of the completion processes—namely, fracing. The global supply and demand for oil, how that affects the price per barrel, and the effect this has on our daily lives are some other issues you may feel more prepared and willing to discuss once you have a basic understanding of the industry.

This book will also be useful if you are interested in the oil and gas industry as a potential career choice. Learning about the various parts of the upstream oil and gas process may trigger an interest in a particular area that you can then research further.

Finally, if you are an industry person who works in only one area of the business, this book is for you, too. My experience in the oil and gas industry has shown me that, too often, people working in the business tend to stay within their area(s) of expertise and become caught up in the silos of their profession. Other than in some very expensive courses, there is really no place where you can find information about the total exploration and upstream process. Having an understanding of that total process and how your job fits into it will help you become better in your role. An improved understanding of the entire upstream process will also provide the basis for better dialogue between various groups that may be in conflict, whether they be within the industry, within a company, or external to the industry. This of course, assumes that people are open to learning new ideas and want to try to understand the issues from both sides of a conflict. An example of a potential conflict within a company is when a group responsible for delivering an increase in reserves wants to immediately move forward with drilling activity to meet their targets, but the steps required for drilling to start have not been completed due to the complexities involved with either landowner or environmental issues. An example of where there could be conflict between the industry and external parties is when construction of a major pipeline is proposed. One group sees a long-term need for the pipeline and the other group does not see that need. An understanding of the issues from both sides of the conflict may help to resolve some of the contentious issues.

As an aside to my technical colleagues, I am not trying with this book to oversimplify your jobs or make light of what you do. Rather, I am attempting to explain what you do in easy-to-understand terms so that others can gain an appreciation for the complexities of your various jobs and how you contribute to the upstream process. We all have a piece of the puzzle that makes up the upstream part of the industry.

About Me

Even though I have lived in Calgary, Alberta (the energy capital of Canada), since I was a year old, I basically knew nothing about the oil and gas industry when I was growing up. Following the completion of my Bachelor of Science degree from the University of Calgary, majoring in biology and psychology, I was fortunate to get a summer job that led to a part-time position that introduced me to the technical side of the oil and gas industry. I was again fortunate while completing my Bachelor of Commerce degree, as I received two job offers: a Junior Geophysicist position with the firm I was working for at the time and a Junior Landman position with a major integrated oil and gas firm. I chose to be a landman because I felt it was a good opportunity to combine my interest in the technical aspects of the oil and gas industry with my interest in the people side of the business. It was a good choice for me, as I have had the opportunity to blend people skills with technical skills.

I have spent my entire career of over thirty-six years working as a landman in the upstream portion of the oil and gas industry. Along the way, I have learned a lot about the technical side of the business by asking many questions and then translating the answers I received into thoughts and ideas that made sense to me. I have had exposure to many of the processes involved in the upstream phase in my work at large multinational companies and in small start-up companies. I would like to share my experiences with you.

I am not a geologist or engineer, but I have been exposed to and understand a fair bit about what these professionals do in their everyday jobs, and some of these tasks are extremely complex. I believe I have the ability to make the complex simple, and I want to apply that skill to explain the upstream process to both industry and non-industry people.

There is more information about me and my background in the Introduction section of my first book, *Mineral Land Rights: What You Need to Know*, as well as on my website, www.levonnelouie.com. Throughout the current book are references to my first book in various topic areas, particularly those generally involving an introduction to how companies are organized within the oil and gas industry and specifically involving land rights.

While my first book was primarily targeted toward landowners and others wanting to know about an essential piece of the oil and gas industry—land—this book is targeted toward a wider audience interested in the upstream oil and gas process, whether they are in the industry or not. I am moving from one subject area in the oil and gas industry to the many topics that encompass the upstream side of the business.

1

Sciences

MANY OF US are familiar with the three basic fields within the study of science from our high school days: biology, chemistry, and physics. Each of these three major sciences has a role to play in the exploration phase of the oil and gas industry. Geology encompasses all three major sciences. Geophysics includes aspects of physics. And engineering incorporates both chemistry and physics. Before you skip this section because "you were never good in science," bear with me; I'm going to try to explain these key disciplines of the oil and gas industry in a simple manner that even non-scientists will understand. Geology and geophysics are the subjects of this chapter, while engineering is covered in Chapters 3 and 4.

Geology

As with many things, the search for oil and gas often starts in the minds of people. Most often, these are people who have studied the solid and liquid parts of the earth, the history of the earth, and how the different processes that formed the earth may have led to an environment that allowed for the creation of various minerals and hydrocarbons on our planet. While many people who study the earth are known as earth scientists, the ones most often involved in searching for minerals or oil and gas are usually known as geologists, and the science they focus on is called geology.

How are the sciences we know as biology, chemistry, and physics related to geology? Biology is important, since it is the study of organisms, whether microbiological, plant, or animal. It is generally believed that much of oil and gas is formed from the remains of organisms. Chemistry is an important part of geology, because the elements of hydrogen and carbon are important to the molecular structure of oil and gas. The forces studied in physics, such as pressure and temperature, and the impact they have on the formation of hydrocarbons are why this branch of science is important to the study of geology.

THREE BASIC TYPES OF ROCKS

At its most basic level, geology is the study of rocks, which are made up of minerals. These minerals and the rocks they form make up the crust of the earth. There are three basic types of rocks in the earth's crust: igneous, sedimentary, and metamorphic.

Igneous rocks are a result of the cooling of liquid rock from deep within the core of the earth. This liquid rock is known as magma if it is below the surface of the earth and lava if it is above the surface. Sedimentary rocks are formed by a mechanical process known as weathering, by a chemical process, or by the accumulation of organic debris. Sedimentary rocks are classified according to the physical features of the rock—such as its texture and mineral composition—rather than where it is from. Metamorphic rocks are formed from igneous or sedimentary rocks that have been changed by temperature, pressure, and/or chemical activity into something completely different. For example, marble is a metamorphic rock from limestone, and quartzite is a metamorphic rock from sandstone. Only sedimentary rocks are considered to have potential as reservoir rocks for oil and gas, because igneous and metamorphic rocks have very few empty spaces within them for oil and gas. The focus of this geology discussion will therefore be on sedimentary rocks.

CLASSIFICATIONS OF SEDIMENTARY ROCKS

There are lots of different types of sedimentary rocks and many different ways to classify them. You could look at physical characteristics such as texture. You could look at the types of minerals contained in the rocks, such as silica or quartz. You could consider the environment in which the sedimentary rocks are deposited and the physical, chemical, and biological conditions that existed at a particular time in that place.

If classifying rocks by their texture, some of the terms used are clastic or detrital, which describe rocks made up of broken pieces or grains of older weathered or eroded rocks that have been deposited in some fashion. This basically means that the rock is an aggregate or collection of mineral grains or rock particles. The pieces could be poorly sorted, with different-sized particles within the rock, or they could be very well sorted. For example, sandstone contains particles that are mainly sand-sized. The size of the particles is another component of texture; the classification of rock size can range from a boulder at one end of the scale toward a pebble and then to a fine sand or clay particle at the other end. Another way of considering the texture of a rock is how dense the rock is. Sedimentary rocks that are mostly made of silt or clay particles are said to have a dense texture. If a rock contains a lot of crystal, it may be referred to as having a crystalline texture.

If you try to classify rocks by the minerals contained in them, you could look at rocks that contain a lot of silica, which would show up as quartz grains. A non-crystalline form of silica could also show up in rocks; this is called chert. Minerals such as calcite and dolomite are major components of limestone and dolomites. Limestone could also contain shell fragments made up of calcite. Another important type of mineral present in sedimentary rocks is clay; an example is kaolinite. The clay particles, in combination with other minerals, can form a cement for the other particles within the rock.

Another way to classify sedimentary rocks is to look at the environment in which they were originally deposited. I personally prefer this method of classification, as I can visualize the environment and compare it to what we see today. Some of the environments are flood plains, alluvial fans, glacial deposits, deltas, shoreline reefs, shallow marine, and deep ocean. If you consider any one of these examples, it is relatively easy to find a setting today that mirrors what the environment would have looked like when the sediments were deposited, then imagine those sediments being covered by thousands of metres of further rock. As sediments are buried, the effects of temperature and pressure begin to turn the animal and plant life buried within the sediments into various hydrocarbons.

RESERVOIR ROCK PROPERTIES

I've already indicated that sedimentary rocks are the primary focus of the oil and gas industry. Some rocks are known as source rocks and others are known primarily as reservoir rocks. Source rocks are so called because they are where oil and gas are actually formed. The components of plant and animal life contained in or around the rock material decompose and, under high pressure and temperature, break down into hydrocarbons, or what we know as oil and gas. Once the oil and gas are formed, they can sometimes move within the spaces in the rocks and come to rest in what are known as reservoir rocks.

Reservoir rocks have certain properties that geologists and engineers within the oil and gas industry must consider. One of the properties is known as porosity, which is the portion of the rock material that is not solid; think of it as the minute pores or holes in the rock. Porosity is important, as it tells us how much space is available in the rock to store gas or fluids. It is important to know not only how much space is available in the rock (known as absolute porosity), but the extent to which these spaces are connected (known as effective porosity). If the spaces are not connected, fluid cannot flow through the rock material.

Permeability is another important reservoir rock property; it is a measure of a rock's ability to transmit fluid. Rocks that are not very permeable are called tight. An example of a highly porous and permeable rock is sandstone. Think about how easily water flows through the sand at a beach. An example of a less porous and impermeable rock is shale. Think about a piece of shale flooring in your home and how difficult it would be for water to flow through it.

A third important reservoir rock property is the fluid saturation of the rock. By looking at cores of the rock, an analysis can be done to find out how much water and oil are in the sample. If the sample has been carefully collected, scientists can also estimate how much gas is in the rock by placing the core in a sealed canister and then measuring how much gas is released into the canister.

With new technology and the ability to produce oil and gas from formations that we couldn't before, the line is blurring between source rocks and reservoir rocks. With production coming out of formations such as shale and coal, which are known as source rocks, we can actually produce from the source instead of taking the chance of producing from a reservoir rock to which oil and gas may or may not have migrated.

WHAT IS A HYDROCARBON?

As the name suggests, a hydrocarbon typically consists of primarily two elements: hydrogen and carbon. Think back to those chemistry days and the periodic table of elements. You may recall your science teacher telling you that hydrogen and carbon are two of the essential elements required for life. Occasionally, hydrocarbons may contain small amounts of oxygen, sulphur, and nitrogen.

The word "hydrocarbon" is sometimes used interchangeably with petroleum, oil, or natural gas. The word "petroleum" actually comes from two Latin words: *petra*, which means rock or stone, and *oleum*, which means oil. Petroleum can exist in solid form, such as when you see it as tar or pitch or as a main component in asphalt, or in liquid form, either crude or refined. Crude oil is what comes out of the ground before it is sent to a refinery.

Many physical properties are used to describe oil, some of which are density, volume, colour, and odor. Liquid petroleum or oil is commonly measured in barrels (imperial system) or cubic metres. There are about 0.159 cubic metres (5.6 cubic feet) of oil in a barrel, and 1 cubic metre (35.3 cubic feet) of oil is about 6.29 barrels.

Natural gas is a lighter form of hydrocarbon. It can be free in the formation pores, dissolved in liquid (think carbonation as in carbonated water or soda), or adsorbed in or attached to a specific rock (think coalbed methane). Natural gas is commonly measured in thousands of cubic metres or feet under a standard set of conditions of pressure and temperature. The reason you need a standard set of conditions is that gas can easily expand. For example, an inflatable ball or balloon at sea level will be a lot softer than the same ball or balloon at the peak of a mountaintop. Similarly, that ball or balloon will be softer on a cold day than on a hot day. There can also be wet gas (contains some fluid in vapour form), dry gas, sweet gas, and sour gas (contains some hydrogen sulphide).

Natural gas is predominantly made up of methane gas, but other hydrocarbon gases may be present, such as ethane. The hydrocarbons might also contain other elements, the most common being oxygen, sulphur, and nitrogen.

HOW HYDROCARBONS ARE FORMED

The focus of oil and gas exploration is to find hydrocarbons in commercial quantities. Traditionally, it was thought that four factors had to be in play: a source rock, a reservoir rock, a suitable trap, and a cap rock over the oil. That is still likely true for oil and gas found in conventional reservoirs. However, as was discussed above, companies are now pursuing unconventional resources such as shale gas and oil and coalbed methane. Rather than trying to figure out where the oil and gas have migrated and how they may have been trapped, geologists can now identify potential source rock and drill directly into it. The hope is that the source rock is not very porous or permeable, as that would mean most resources would have migrated out of it into neighbouring rocks. In these unconventional reservoirs, we are actually drilling into source rocks, such as shale or coal, to find the hydrocarbons, so some of the traditional views do not fully apply to these reservoirs.

However, one question still does apply and that is how hydrocarbons are formed. Most scientists believe that hydrocarbons are formed from organic matter. Large amounts of plant and animal matter are contained in the sedimentary rocks of the earth, and those remains are primarily made up of carbon and hydrogen. Organic matter of marine origin contains the most important plant and animal life when we are talking about exploring for oil and gas.

The only organic matter that becomes source material for hydrocarbons is the material buried and preserved in sediments. Once the material is buried, other factors such as pressure and temperature and possibly bacteria are important to the conversion from plant and animal life to hydrocarbons. If the temperature is too hot, the organic matter will be "cooked"; if it is too cool, the process of degradation and conversion would not happen. Typically, the sediments have to form a protective shield over the plant and animal matter in order to create a source rock. An example of a source rock is shale or coal.

In conventional resources, the oil or gas formed in the tight source rock then has to move to a porous, permeable reservoir rock. This rock could have formed as a result of sand being deposited on top of another rock; an example of a reservoir rock is sandstone.

As more layers of material are deposited on top of the package of sedimentary rocks, thereby creating more pressure, the oil, gas, or water formed by the decayed organic matter escapes from the source rock where it was formed into a neighbouring porous rock. The oil, gas, or water keeps moving until it is somehow trapped. Because of the properties and densities of oil, gas, and water, water will settle on the bottom with oil above it and gas above the oil. Visualize a glass that contains water and oil; you see that the oil floats on top of the water. The same thing happens in the pores of a rock.

TRAPPING HYDROCARBONS

A trap is simply something that either stops the free movement of oil within a rock or concentrates the oil in a limited area. There are two main types of traps: structural and stratigraphic.

A structural trap is a result of some form of physical change to the earth's crust that extends down through the layers of sedimentary rock. An example of a structural trap is a fold, where the layers of rocks have bent. Although it is hard to imagine that something as seemingly solid as rock could bend, a tremendous horizontal (and sometimes vertical) force, likely over a period of time, can cause rock to bend and fold. An anticline is a type of fold where the beds are convex or bent upward. A syncline is a type of fold where the layers are concave or bent downward.

Another type of structural trap is a dome, a symmetrical uplifting of the beds that results in the layers dipping away from the top of the dome in all directions. Domes can be created from upwardly moving masses of material from deep in the earth. This could be a substance like rock salt, thereby creating the salt domes in the Gulf of Mexico, or molten rock moving upward.

People who live on the west coast of North America are familiar with another common structural trap known as a fault. This is a fracture in the rock where there has been movement parallel to the break or up and down at the break. The movement can be fractions of a centimetre or thousands of metres. People living on the west coast of North America often experience earthquakes when there is movement along these faults. Deep in the sediments of the earth, some faults have caused one side of the break to be hundreds of metres higher than the opposite side of the break. Even though the present industry focus may have shifted to drilling into and producing from unconventional resources, it is still important to understand concepts such as faults, as they will have an impact on where an oil company decides to drill.

Stratigraphic traps are caused when a very porous, permeable rock is overlain or surrounded by a less permeable and less porous rock. Because the oil cannot penetrate this neighbouring layer, it becomes trapped against the boundary between the two formations. A classic example of a stratigraphic trap is a reef. This is any dome-like mass built exclusively by sea organisms such as algae and coral. The reef is then buried and enclosed in rock containing different minerals. Other common stratigraphic traps are lenses of sand, offshore bars, and river channels.

I personally find it easier to visualize stratigraphic traps, as I can see them in the present world. Think about your last trip to a tropical paradise and the diving or snorkelling you did around a coral reef. If you haven't had a chance to do that, think about photos you may have seen of the Great Barrier

Reef off the coast of Australia. You will recall that it is teeming with animal and plant life. Now imagine burying that reef under thousands of metres of sediments and waiting a few million years as oil or gas are created and captured in that reef.

Similarly, think about the last time you had a chance to stroll at the seashore or along the banks of a river. You may have seen sandbars just off the beach or in the middle of the river. You may have also seen tidal pools containing a lot of interesting creatures in among the sandbars. Now imagine that area being buried under thousands of metres of sediment. I think you may be able to understand how it is easier for me to visualize stratigraphic traps.

Trapping mechanisms are not always just structural or stratigraphic; often they are a combination of both. There is also the effect of erosion (often wind or water or both) on the rocks after they have been deposited. This creates a boundary known as an unconformity. After erosion, further deposits of sediments could have covered the unconformity boundary.

The following figures illustrate a fault, an anticline and a syncline, a reef, and a lens in cross-section.

Figure 1: Example of one type of fault

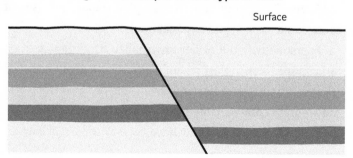

Sciences   23

Figure 2: Anticline and syncline

Surface

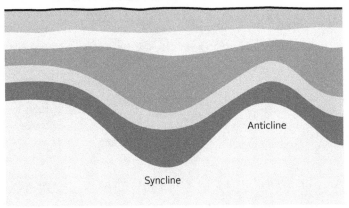

Anticline

Syncline

Figure 3: Simplified view of a reef

Slice down through the earth:

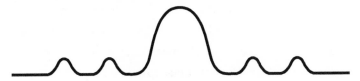

There may be accumulations of oil or gas at the tops of the reefs.

Aerial view looking down over four sections
of land showing the tops of the reefs:

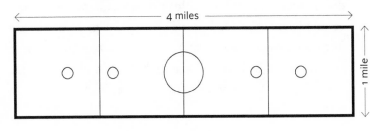

Figure 4: Lenses of sand

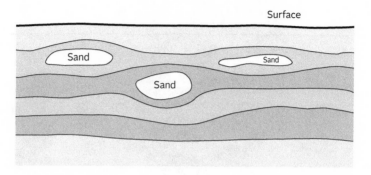

GEOLOGISTS' ROLE IN THE EXPLORATION PROCESS

Now that you've learned a little about the science of geology and how it relates to the oil and gas industry, let's look at what a geologist must do in the exploration process.

Geologists working in the early days of the oil and gas industry began with an idea or concept of where there might be oil and gas based on a model of what the earth may have looked like millions of years ago. Today, in areas with existing oil and gas production, geologists often expand on ideas and concepts generated by other geologists before them.

In addition to knowing about different types of rocks, geologists need to understand what the environment looked like in past climates to create the rocks we see today. As discussed earlier in this geology section, an important part of this is trying to determine what plant and animal life (including micro-organisms) might have existed in these past climates. By knowing where these creatures may have existed, what was surrounding them, and what may have happened to the area over time, geologists try to predict where we might find oil and gas.

Geologists also need to understand the trapping mechanisms in the area they are studying. Remember that with conventional resources, we need a source rock, a reservoir rock, and a trapping mechanism. There is no sense in drilling a well where the geologist believes the environment was good for the formation of oil or gas but not for the creation of a trapping mechanism; with nothing to trap it, the oil or gas will have migrated somewhere else.

Geologists try to create a three-dimensional picture of what the earth looks like below the surface that we see. They do this by creating maps using data points from the boundaries or surface of a formation that may be several hundreds or thousands of metres below the surface. Many data points might be available, particularly if earlier drilling activity has reached the formation, or there may be very few data points if the formation is a relatively new exploration target with few penetrations.

The data points are derived from the tops of formations that are identified or "picked" from the records, known as logs, of wells that have been drilled in the past. These well logs are available to the industry from commercial vendors and are available in different formats. Once various values are extracted from these well logs and plotted onto a map, the geologist begins the "art of contouring."

A contour line is a line joining points of equal value. These points can represent any number of things such as pressure, porosity, permeability, thickness, and elevation. I call it the "art of contouring" because, given a piece of paper with a number of data points on it, different individuals with different terms of reference will likely produce quite different contour maps. While computer contouring programs can assist the geologist, the resulting maps depend on the inputs that the geologist provides. I know many veteran geologists who still prefer to pick up a pencil and use their own creativity to tweak a computer-generated map.

Using the available data points, geologists can create maps showing various things. Two common maps are a structure map and an isopach map. A structure map is very similar to a topographic map that you might use when planning a hike. Both the structure map and a common topographic map might use sea level as a reference point. A big difference is that the structure map will show the ups and downs of the surface of a formation deep below the earth's crust.

An isopach map shows the thickness of a particular formation. Thick and thin areas may give some clues on various structural and stratigraphic traps.

To provide a more complete picture, geologic maps must be accompanied by geologic cross-sections. The geologic maps show the conditions that exist in the horizontal plane, while geologic cross-sections show the structure and stratigraphy in the vertical dimension. The structural cross-section has a constant elevation as its reference point. The most obvious elevation to use is sea level, but it can be any elevation. For a stratigraphic cross-section, a geologist picks a common formation in the area and uses the top or bottom of that formation as its constant elevation. Any ups and downs in the formations below it are all relative to the reference formation. The objective is to see how the sediments may have been deposited or to see changes in those depositional patterns.

The geologist picks the wells that are to be placed on the line of the cross-section and the orientation of the section lines in relation to the basin being examined. You need both geologic mapping and geologic cross-sections to get as complete a picture as possible of the geology of the area. With this picture, the geologist is in a better position to recommend which land should be acquired and where a well should be drilled on the land.

Geophysics

Another area of earth sciences that applies to the oil and gas industry is geophysics, which is the study of the physics of the earth. Geophysics includes the fields of seismology, magnetism, gravity, radioactivity, hydrology, meteorology, geodesy, volcanology, and oceanography.

The area of geophysics most commonly used in the search for oil and gas is seismology, which is essentially the study of waves and how they travel through the earth. As I wrote in *Mineral Land Rights*,

> Many people are familiar with the waves that occur when the tide is coming in or going out. A few people are familiar with the waves that occur when an earthquake hits a

region and causes waves on the surface of the earth or water (sometimes resulting in tsunamis).

Even fewer people are aware of the waves that occur when an energy source at the surface of the earth creates a vibration that then travels down through the various layers of the earth; this is what seismologists study. The different compositions of the various layers in the earth will allow these waves of energy to either pass through a particular layer (possibly bending the wave as it passes through) or bounce off the layer. The different compositions of the layers also affect the speed of these waves. The energy reflected back to the surface is recorded, and using various mathematical formulas and computer programs, a geophysicist generates a picture of what the layers below the surface might look like. A seismic program would consist of a number of energy discharges and multiple receivers to record the energy being returned to the surface. Different types of energy sources are used, but traditionally, small shots of dynamite are placed in small holes drilled into the ground [vibration pads are also used to create the energy source]—hence the industry phrase of "shooting" a seismic program.

Figure 5 shows a simple picture of what happens when seismic is shot in an area.

Geophysics is not always used on an exploration prospect (sometimes referred to as a "play" or "play type"), but it can be helpful in understanding what the subsurface looks like. Working with the geologist, geophysicists may be able to

Figure 5: Simplified view of what happens during one piece (or one shot) of a seismic program

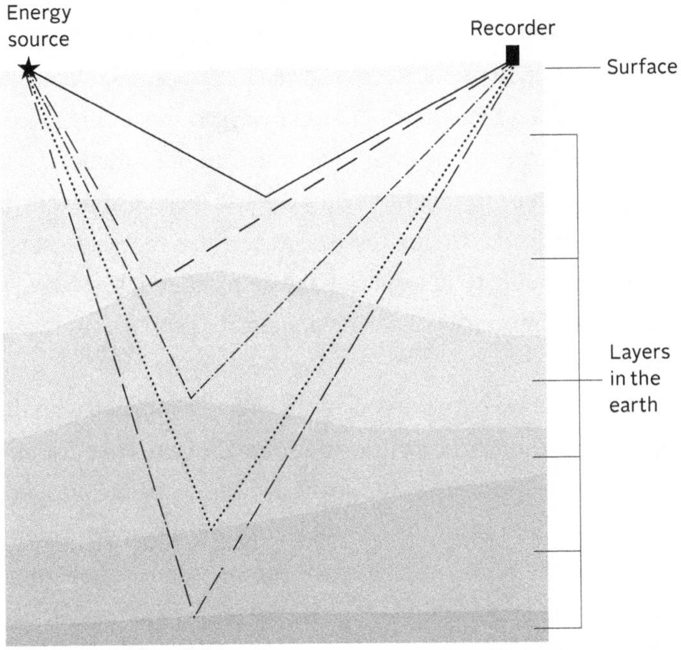

This diagram shows one energy source and one recorder or receiver, known as a geophone. However, there are actually multiple recorders for each energy source. A seismic program would have multiple energy sources. The result: a lot of data that can be processed and manipulated by computers.

visualize different traps on their seismic lines. For example, geophysics would be very helpful in an area that is sparsely drilled but in which the geologist suspects there are a lot of faults. The results can help identify the location of the faults, which will likely influence the location of the wells to be drilled.

As computing power increases, the number of tools that geophysicists have also increases. Some claim to be able to tell whether there is oil or gas in a formation. However, it is important to recognize that what a geophysicist sees is simply the result of computer manipulations and may not be real. Geophysicists are always looking at different ways to shoot energy into the ground and to record it to get the most information from shooting a seismic program. They are also looking at new ways to process the data to improve the picture that results. Cost is a consideration both in acquiring the data and in interpreting it. As with any professional, the reputation of a geophysicist is very important.

Now that we have the geologist's picture combined with the geophysicist's picture, we have to acquire the land so we can drill. With all due respect to my geologist and geophysicist colleagues, no matter how good their models may be, it's impossible to know if there is oil and/or gas that can be produced economically and efficiently until the land rights are acquired and we are able to drill a well.

Key Points in This Chapter

- The main group of earth scientists who search for oil and gas are known as geologists, and they are sometimes supported by geophysicists.

- Three basic types of rock form the earth's crust: igneous, sedimentary, and metamorphic. Only sedimentary rocks have the potential to act as source rocks or reservoir rocks for oil and gas.

- Sedimentary rocks can be classified in many ways, including the texture of the rocks, the content of the minerals in the rocks, or the environment in which the sedimentary rocks have been deposited.

- Sedimentary rocks can be source rocks or reservoir rocks. In the case of unconventional oil and gas resources, sedimentary rocks are often both source rocks and the reservoir rocks.

- Hydrocarbons are composed primarily of the elements hydrogen and carbon. The most common belief is that they are formed by deposits of organic matter (plant and animal) that have been covered by other sediments. Under high pressure and temperature and sometimes assisted by bacterial activity, the organic matter changes to hydrocarbons.

- Hydrocarbons need to be trapped in order to be a potential commercial hydrocarbon deposit. Traps can be structural, stratigraphic, or a combination of both.

- Geophysicists study the physics of the earth. This branch of earth sciences includes seismology, magnetism, gravity, radioactivity, hydrology, meteorology, geodesy, volcanology, and oceanography. The area used most often in the exploration for hydrocarbons is seismology.

- Geologists, using various data organized into maps and cross-sections, and sometimes with the help of geophysicists, try to create as complete a three-dimensional picture as possible of what lies beneath the surface of the earth so they can predict where oil and gas may be found in commercial quantities. Even though geologists may create an elaborate and complex model, we do not know if there is oil and gas in commercial quantities until we drill.

2

Land

ONCE THE EARTH scientists have determined where exploration for hydrocarbons should focus, an oil and gas company needs to secure the land rights, both mineral and surface, in order to drill a well.

Mineral Rights

As a landman, I'm charged with the task of acquiring mineral land rights for companies, but I always prefer that geologists identify where we should focus the acquisition process. I can acquire many hectares of mineral rights at very reasonable prices, but without a geologist's direction, I may be leasing a lot of moose pasture.

My previous book, *Mineral Land Rights: What You Need to Know,* describes in great detail the different types of land rights, the things a landowner can do with those rights, and the considerations when land is leased. The book also describes drilling spacing units and how much land must be leased to get a well licence to drill a well. In addition, there is a section describing the various types of agreements that companies negotiate with other companies in order to secure the rights to drill on a parcel of land. Therefore, I will not spend a lot of time on this topic except to reinforce that it is necessary to secure both the mineral land and the surface of the land in order to drill a well. The best geological idea or model or the best drilling or completion practices won't matter if a company does not have the land, as it won't be able to drill to test its concept.

Land ownership can be a complex subject. There are mineral rights and surface rights, and either of these rights can be held by the government (in Canada these lands are typically known as Crown lands) or by individual people or companies (typically known as freehold or fee simple lands). Leases for the mineral rights or surface rights or both can be secured from the Crown or freehold owners. Sometimes, in order to drill one well, a company needs to secure rights from multiple parties with a mixture of Crown and freehold leases. In addition, if another company has already leased a portion or all of the lands necessary to drill a well, it may be necessary to negotiate an agreement with that company in order to acquire the lands.

The first piece of land that has to be secured is the mineral land. A company will want to lease not only the minerals on the land where the geologist wants to drill, but as much land as possible on the geologist's entire prospect. If the company has success when drilling the well, it will want the ability to drill additional, hopefully successful, wells on the same prospect. There is no point leasing only the land required to prove a geologist's concept if another company is able to follow up on a successful well by drilling on the adjoining land because you haven't tied it up first.

If the land adjoining the target drilling site is not leased to someone else, a company will likely want to secure the lease(s) before it drills the first well. If the landowners have already leased the mineral rights to another company, the first company will likely try to negotiate a deal in order to drill on the adjoining lands either before or after drilling on the original lands it has leased. (A company may drill on lands leased by another company before it drills on lands it has leased if the location of the other company's lands will, in the eyes of a geologist, be a better place to test the concept.)

What if a geologist selects a prospect where there are no lands available to lease—that is, if all the lands on the prospect have already been leased by other companies? If the prospect the geologist wants to test is different than what is already producing on those lands, an approach can be made to one of the other companies to drill a well in order to test the geologist's concept; in exchange, the company doing the drilling will earn an interest in the lands. In the oil and gas industry, this is known as a farmout or a farmin, depending on which side of the deal one is on.

I can acquire mineral rights by leasing them directly from the landowner(s), by negotiating a deal with another company that has already leased the rights, or both. If I can tie up the adjoining land and the first well is successful, my company will be able to continue drilling and developing the land. How much land I need to secure before my company is ready to drill often depends on the type of hydrocarbon (oil or gas) being pursued, whether it is a conventional or unconventional resource, and how big the budget is. The minimum amount of mineral rights I have to lease or control is the drilling spacing unit that is designated by the regulator. In western Canada, this has typically been one section (256 hectares/640 acres) for a gas well and one quarter section (64 hectares/160 acres) for an oil well.

Personally, if my budget would allow it and I could negotiate the deals in a logical fashion, I would like to tie up all the land covered by a geologist's prospect before drilling begins. That is not often the case, so I, the geologist, and my company have to decide on the minimum amount of land to be secured before we decide to move forward with drilling. Various factors are considered, such as the cost of the well, probability of success, expected production, and ultimate reserves. For example, if the cost of the well is millions of dollars, I would likely want to secure more land before I drill, since I would want to make sure that the company can follow up the expected success with other wells to develop the prospect.

Surface Rights

Once I secure the minimum mineral land rights I feel comfortable with (which is usually more than the minimum designated by the regulator), I need to secure surface access before I can apply for a drilling licence for a well. Whereas a regulated drilling spacing unit requires my company to have a minimum amount of mineral rights under our control to apply for a well licence, a surface lease can be much smaller, as I need to lease only the surface rights necessary to conduct the intended operations. I may need a roadway (usually fifteen metres/fifty feet wide) and a rectangular or square area large enough to bring in a drilling rig and the equipment required to drill the well, test it, complete it, and tie it in (which means connecting the well to a pipeline system that gathers the hydrocarbons from the area and transports them to a processing facility). So while I need a minimum of 256 hectares (640 acres) of mineral rights to drill a gas well or 64 hectares (160 acres) to drill an oil well, the surface lease could be less than 1 hectare (2.5 acres) if I don't need a roadway or up to 2 or 3 hectares (5 to 7 acres), depending on how big the required wellsite is and how long the roadway is.

With some resource plays, multiple horizontal wells are drilled from one surface location, sometimes referred to as a pad or padsite. A padsite for multiple wells is often quite a bit bigger than a wellsite for a single well. For example, the area required for a wellsite to drill a single well might be 1 hectare (2.5 acres), whereas a lease for a padsite might be 6 hectares (15 acres). The padsite would allow a company to drill a number of wells—perhaps six to ten wells. This allows companies to drill and access the resource while minimizing the impact on the surface of the land and the surface landowner, as the company does not have to secure six to ten leases to access the same resource.

Sometimes, at the same time as securing a lease to cover the wellsite and access road, the surface land agent may also approach the landowner for a Right-of-Way Agreement or easement. This assumes that the well will be successful in terms of finding hydrocarbons that can be produced commercially. A Right-of-Way Agreement allows the company to lay a pipeline to move the production from the section of land in which the well has been drilled to a gathering system that will take the hydrocarbons to a central processing facility. Other times, a company will wait until the well has proven to be successful before approaching the landowner for a Right-of-Way Agreement or easement. The timing of the approach to the landowner depends on many factors, such as the probability of success and how difficult it is to deal with that particular landowner.

Public Consultations and Impact Assessments

Besides negotiating a surface lease with the surface landowner, the surface land agent is often required to notify other landowners in the area who may be impacted by the proposed operation. These could be other surface landowners in the area or any tenants who are renting, for example, a house or farming or grazing land from the surface landowner(s). This activity is often referred to as the public consultation process.

An example of when extensive public consultation may be required is when there is the possibility that hydrogen sulphide (H_2S) gas will be encountered in either the target formation or other formations through which the company will be drilling to reach the target formation. Hydrogen sulphide is extremely dangerous at high concentrations or even at small concentrations over an extended period. Regulations dictate the minimum area within which all owners and residents must be notified and that there be an emergency plan in the event of an accidental release of H_2S. Each company typically has a standard plan for such an emergency, but part of the consultation process involves customizing the standard plan for this specific well. For example, a customized plan will likely include a list of the owners and residents within the designated radius of the wellsite and their emergency contact information.

A simpler consultation process may involve contacting residences downwind of a well or contacting a company that has a nearby business to advise them of the upcoming activity. Sometimes an oil and gas company will go above and beyond what is required by legislation/regulation in order to be a good neighbour, particularly if it is expecting to operate in an area for a long time.

Depending on the area in which the work is to be done, an archaeological assessment or a wildlife assessment may be required. In both cases, the idea is to identify if anything, such as artifacts or a species at risk, needs to be identified and protected. For example, in areas where there may have been early settlements, items of archaeological significance may need to be preserved.

In the case of a wildlife assessment, either animals in the area or their habitat might need to be protected. For example, burrowing owls, an endangered species under the Canadian

Species at Risk Act, may be present. Sometimes the findings of these assessments can result in lengthy delays for the company wanting to drill a well or even cancellation of a well location. In that case, the company will have to find a different location to test its concept.

An environmental impact assessment may also be required. This is almost always necessary for projects that cover a large area, but also required any time there is the potential for a project to have an impact on the environment. Covering all aspects of the environment—land, water, and air—such an assessment considers the possibility and probability of environmental contamination from the project, the type of contamination, and the mitigating steps to be taken to reduce or eliminate the risk of contamination. This assessment must be submitted, reviewed, and approved before licences for the project are granted.

The consultation processes discussed so far mainly affect the surface of the land. However, another type of consultation that may be required for surface and/or mineral rights is First Nations or Aboriginal consultation. This is the case when a company is working in an area that may have been used for the traditional activities (such as hunting, trapping, and fishing) of a First Nation and their ancestors. Even when the mineral and surface rights are held by the government (which is often the case), consultation with the First Nation(s) in the area is still required. This consultation involves issuing a notification of the activities to be conducted and likely holding a series of meetings where parties can address questions and concerns about the activities and the impact they may have on the traditional activities of the First Nation(s).

In some areas, consultations may need to be held with more than one First Nation community, as there is the potential for overlapping traditional areas. Conducting an appropriate and effective consultation is becoming more and more important, as this "duty to consult" has recently been confirmed by Canadian courts and the consultation process has received more media attention in the past several years. Many of the large projects being proposed include the necessity to consult with multiple First Nation communities.

Once the mineral land and surface land have been acquired, a company can apply to the appropriate regulator for a licence to drill the well. While the mineral and surface land departments may supply some of the information for the well licence application, the drilling department within an oil and gas company usually has responsibility for this function due to the detailed technical information that needs to be provided. For example, the regulator will want to know the target formation the company is pursuing, how deep the company is planning to drill, and what steps it will take to protect the environment.

Key Points in This Chapter

- There is a difference between mineral land rights and surface land rights.

- Mineral rights and surface rights can be held by either the government (commonly known as the Crown in Canada) or individual persons or corporations. While the owner of the mineral rights on a parcel of land could also own the surface rights on that same parcel, this is often not the case in settled areas. A company may have to deal with multiple parties to secure the rights by way of leases.

- For tactical reasons, a company may want to secure more than the minimum amount of mineral land rights required by the regulator to apply for a licence to drill a well.

- Typically, mineral leases cover more lands than surface leases.

- Besides negotiating with the landowner, many different assessments and/or consultations may be required to secure the surface rights before a licence to drill is granted. For example, a company may be required to conduct public consultations, archaeological assessments, wildlife assessments, environmental impact assessments, and First Nations consultations.

- A company must secure both mineral and surface land rights before it can apply for a licence to drill a well.

3

Engineers' World: Operations

MANY TYPES OF engineers can gravitate toward many different areas within the oil and gas industry, depending on their interests and skills, because so many different activities in this business require their expertise.

For example, engineers may become involved on the operations side of oil and gas exploration; that can range from overseeing the drilling of wells to operating or managing the wells after they start producing. Engineers responsible for drilling coordinate the pre-drilling activities, the actual drilling of the well, and, if successful, the steps necessary to put the well into production. At this point, the well is typically turned over to an operations group to make sure that conditions remain optimized for maximum production from the well. As I have said earlier in this book, it doesn't matter how good the maps and models are or how much land a company is able to acquire; the only way to find oil and gas is to drill for them.

Licensing, Site Preparation, and Construction

Once the landmen and land agents have secured the mineral rights and the surface rights required for the project and have conducted all necessary consultations, the drilling department is ready to apply for a well licence. Most jurisdictions have regulatory bodies that oversee the many regulations that govern the drilling of an oil and gas well to ensure that the drilling operations are conducted in a safe manner. A lot of information is required on a well licence application, including the surface location of the hole, the ultimate bottomhole location (the end or bottom of the hole, which may intentionally not be directly below the surface location), survey coordinates, and target formation(s) and depth(s). As discussed in Chapter 2 in the section about consultation requirements, the regulator often asks if all necessary consultations have been completed and whether the applicant has all the mineral and surface rights required to conduct the operation and the working interest ownership of the well.

Once a company receives a well licence from the regulator (or sometimes before it receives the well licence), it will start to "move dirt" on the surface lease to construct its wellsite and access road. If the well is deep and requires a lot of equipment on-site, the topsoil will be stripped off the site and preserved (and often laid along the edges of the site). This is as important to the company doing the work as it is to the landowners. Assuming that the well is a success, once production has been exhausted from the well, the site needs to be reclaimed so that vegetation can grow on the site. The vegetation needs to be as close to the original as possible before the regulator will grant a reclamation certificate. In some jurisdictions, the surface lease can be surrendered only when a reclamation certificate is granted. In the past, soil was simply pushed to the side without consideration for the layers of topsoil. Experience showed that crops did not grow as well in these disturbed areas as they did in the surrounding field. Now the topsoil layers are carefully stripped and then replaced in a similar order. This gives the crops or vegetation the best chance of coming back to their pre-disturbed levels.

When the target formation is very shallow, sometimes the company will construct a "minimum disturbance" site. This is exactly what the words describe. Very little disturbance is made to the site; if possible, even the layers of soil are not disturbed.

Many of us may not think about layers of topsoil, even if we are gardeners, but have you ever had to drill a hole to put in a fence post? You may remember that the first part of the drilling was relatively easy as you went through the top fifteen to thirty centimetres (six to twelve inches). In new subdivisions, this would typically be the layers of topsoil provided by the developer or builder, and the depth would depend on how generous they were. Depending on your soil, you may have noticed that the soil was very black and appeared to be rich in organic matter. You may even have found that the next half metre still consisted of good, black dirt even though it was more compact than the top layers. At some point, the drilling likely became harder (especially if you were using a hand auger) as you entered a clay layer, and harder still as you entered a layer containing a lot of rocks and boulders. When you finally finished drilling those sometimes frustrating, but necessary, fence post holes, you may recall looking down and seeing layers of earth in the hole. Now imagine drilling a well over a thousand metres deep, and you can imagine how many layers you would encounter.

Drilling

One of the main purposes of drilling is to drill a hole to the prospective formation to see if there is any prospectivity for oil and gas; that is, are there hydrocarbons present? Other goals are to drill without any problems and to stay on budget—which isn't always the case. If no hydrocarbons are found, the well must be abandoned and the site reclaimed. Generally, there are very strict rules and regulations to guide what must happen to a wellbore when it is abandoned.

Once a company has decided to drill a well, the drilling engineer is often tasked with negotiating a contract with a drilling contractor to physically drill the well. Large companies may have their own drilling rigs, but that is now rare. Depending on the type of well to be drilled, the economy, and the availability (supply and demand) of rigs, the contract could contain a day rate or a meterage (footage) rate. A company would also negotiate for the ancillary services and products associated with or used during the drilling, such as drilling muds, tools, bits, water, etc.

Rigs are many and varied and are sometimes built for specific purposes. There is a very basic difference between a cable tool rig and a rotary rig. Using a cable tool rig is like pounding a nail in with a hammer. Using a rotary rig is like putting a screw in with a screwdriver. While the cable tool method of drilling was sometimes used in the past, the rotary method is now used almost exclusively in western Canada. The depth that a drilling rig can drill to is a key factor, as is the type of well it is designed to drill (e.g., vertical, slant, directional, horizontal).

A rotary rig has four basic components. The first is the component that produces or transmits power. The second is the hoisting component used to lift the pipes that make up the drilling casing string and the tubing. The third is the rotating component that allows the drill bit to drill the hole. These first three components are all located above the surface of the ground and they help to make a hole. Sometimes the bottomhole location can be several thousand metres below the surface and hundreds or thousands of metres away laterally from the surface location.

The fourth component is a mud system, critical to drilling a deep hole. The mud has many functions. It provides lubrication for drilling, it keeps the drill bit cool, and it helps to lift and remove the drill cuttings from the hole. The mud also provides hydrostatic pressure in the hole to prevent any fluids or gases in the formations from entering the hole and causing what is called a blowout. Mud also helps to form a film or layer against the walls of the hole to prevent the walls from caving in, and it supports the weight of the drill pipe by adding some buoyancy. During the drilling operation, the mud is continuously circulated; when the circulation stops, the mud will gel and hold the drill cuttings in suspension.

Think again about drilling those fence post holes. Did you ever experience frustration because the hole kept caving in (especially near the top) as you were trying to drill it? Do you recall adding a bit of water to the hole so that the dirt clumped together so you could pull it out of the hole? You didn't want to add too much water, or the mud would become too runny and the dirt wouldn't clump.

This is a similar idea to drilling mud, though drilling mud is much more complex and can be a science. As a well is being drilled, tests are run on the mud to make sure it stays in good condition. Mud can be one of the most expensive parts of the drilling operation, as it is critical to the success and safety of the operation.

Rather than simply a combination of water and dirt, as in the case of simple fence post holes, drilling mud is a mixture of water, a gel made up of bentonite (an absorbent clay mineral), various minerals such as barites, and other compounds such as lignosulfonates. (Lignosulfonates are a by-product of the production of wood pulp and help to reduce the viscosity of the mud.) Ultimately, the purpose is to create a mud that has enough weight (measured in kilograms per litre or pounds per gallon) to create enough pressure in the wellbore so that formation fluids do not enter the wellbore and potentially cause a blowout while drilling. However, the mud engineers need to be careful not to make the mud so heavy that it pushes the oil and gas deeper into the formation (known as damaging the formation). Mud truly is a science, as other factors such as viscosity, acidity, water loss, and availability of clay to cake the walls of the wellbore to prevent sloughing must all be taken into consideration.

One term used frequently in the oil and gas industry is the "spud date" of a well. It can take a long time to construct the lease and set up the equipment to drill the well once a company is on the wellsite. Often, it is necessary to know when a well started, and that has to have some consistency. For example, if there is a contractual obligation to start operations by a certain date, what does "starting operations" mean? This ambiguity created the need for a defined date and time for when things start, and we often refer to having to "spud" a well by a certain date, or "spudding in" a well. When this term is used, everyone in the industry knows that this is when the drill bit is "turning to the right" or when it is starting to "make hole."

THE WELLSITE GEOLOGIST

While drilling, particularly if it has been really easy to drill through a section of rock, it is possible to drill through a formation that may be capable of producing hydrocarbons. Therefore, the driller generally drills under the direction of a geologist, known as the wellsite geologist, who looks at the rock samples and well cuttings that come up out of the wellbore to try to determine the formations that the drill bit is passing through and to see if there is any evidence of hydrocarbons in the formation(s) being drilled. This wellsite geologist is usually a different person than the geologist who conceived the play, although the exploration geologist may also be on-site at the well as it is being drilled.

As the wellsite geologist examines the drill cuttings brought to the surface by the drilling mud, he or she creates a sample log (also known as a stratigraphic log or geology log). This log is a record of the rock samples taken from the drilling mud and is one of the main sources of information about the rock and fluid properties of the well. The log includes a description of the rock, such as rock type, colour, and crystallinity, along with any qualitative data such as porosity, permeability, and evidence of oil staining. The wellsite geologist also has other tasks, such as picking the location of cores and tests, packing and shipping recovered cores and fluid samples, and deciding which parts of the wellbore should be logged.

FORMATION EVALUATION AND TESTING

Looking at the drill cuttings is one form of formation evaluation, but there are other methods that provide additional data. Each method complements the others in order to evaluate the formations in the well as completely as possible while keeping in mind the economics of drilling the well. Once a target formation is reached, and if it appears that hydrocarbons may be present, the wellsite geologist essentially has three choices: decide that the amounts of hydrocarbon are too small to be produced commercially, cut a core, or call for a drill stem test.

Cutting a core means taking a cylindrical piece of rock out of the ground to examine instead of just looking at the ground-up rock samples that come up with the drilling mud. Cores can be 4.45 to 13.33 centimetres (1.75 to 5.25 inches) in diameter and 0.45 to 121.92 metres (1.5 to 400 feet) long. There are also small cores known as sidewall cores, for which "plugs" from 2.54 to 5.08 centimetres (1 to 2 inches) long and 2.54 to 3.81 centimetres (1 to 1.5 inches) in diameter are taken from the sides of the wellbore at selected intervals.

An obvious advantage of looking at cores is the ability to analyze the porosity, permeability, and fluid content directly on a whole piece of rock rather than having to extrapolate the information from some ground-up samples. The disadvantage is the additional cost and time that it takes to run a core, as all the drill pipe must be pulled out of the hole so that the drilling bit can be replaced with a coring bit (the cost is lower for sidewall cores). Most geologists would like to core every well they drill, as working with the rock directly gives them the best information about the rock; more rock material is always better. However, the additional cost and time mean they have to be selective about which wells they core. The wells chosen may be the initial exploratory wells being drilled into a formation whose surrounding area has no other production. To gather the rest of the geological information, the geologist has to make do with the data they get from drill stem tests (DSTs) from other wells in the general area that may not be in the immediate vicinity of the well being cored.

A DST is run to try to determine if hydrocarbons are present in a formation in a commercially viable quantity. The DST equipment is essentially a collection of valves and pressure sensors. The drill pipe is pulled from the hole and the DST equipment is lowered to the formation of interest. Common types of DST are a bottomhole test, in which the most recently penetrated formation is tested, or a straddle test, in which packers are set below and above a zone of interest. DSTs are run to test the fluid from the zone and to measure pressures.

A packer—a piece of rubber or other material that is slightly smaller than the diameter of the hole and about 76.2

centimetres (30 inches) long—is also lowered into the hole. The packer is positioned so that the formation of interest can be isolated from the formations below (and above, in the case of a straddle test). The rubber packer is expanded so that it seals itself firmly against the walls of the hole. This serves to isolate a portion of the hole from the drilling mud, which is creating hydrostatic pressure against the fluids in the formation. Valves in the test tool are opened, thus reducing the pressure against the formation and allowing the fluids to flow into the test tool. Some of these fluids are examined as they are recovered in the test tool. The test tool is left open for a predetermined amount of time, while the pressure readings from the test tool are examined. Initial and final readings are taken for the hydrostatic pressure, flow pressure, and shut-in pressure. By looking at differences in the pressures, the company can make an educated guess as to whether there are enough hydrocarbons in the formation to allow the well to be produced commercially.

LOGGING

Logging is another process to obtain information about the formations in a well, and it can be done during drilling or when drilling is complete. Many different types of logs can be run depending on what the company wants to measure. Many of the logging tools measure the resistivity and porosity of the rock. These measurements are made relative to the other rocks in the vicinity as the logging tool is moved up the hole.

The early logging tools were based on the principle of how electricity is conducted through a rock. The resistivity of a rock gives us clues about its mineral makeup and whether it contains any fluids. A dry, solid piece of rock will not conduct electricity (with the exception of some rocks, such as graphite, that conduct electricity like metals; graphite-shafted golf clubs conduct electricity just as well as steel-shafted clubs). In addition to resistivity logs, other logs commonly used are spontaneous potential (SP) logs, sonic logs, gamma ray logs, and neutron density logs.

Companies are required to submit copies of all logs run to the regulatory body and they become part of the public record. The log database is a historical record of the rock characteristics measured by logs that scientists can access to compare the log information from one well to another. This helps them to develop their ideas about where oil and gas might be found.

MECHANICS OF DRILLING

This section is for those of you who want to know about the different processes involved in drilling a well and the types of equipment used. This section also covers some of the common terms people use when talking about drilling a well.

Steel pipe, sometimes known as casing, is used for various purposes in the drilling of a well, including to prevent the hole from caving in, to control formation pressures, and to prevent the mixing or communication of fluids between different formations. The casing, which is cemented into place, may be of various diameters depending on where it is used.

The first piece of pipe, known as the conductor pipe or casing, is relatively short (usually less than six metres/twenty feet), is designed to prevent the rim of the recently spudded well from caving in, and can protect shallow water or gas sands. The blowout prevention (sometimes known as the BOP) equipment might also be attached to this piece of pipe.

The second piece of pipe is known as the surface casing, and it can vary in length up to about 25 percent of the projected depth of the hole. This second string of pipe can also be used for blowout protection and to isolate water aquifer sands.

Intermediate casing may be set next, particularly when the hole to be protected is a longer, deeper hole or when there is a need to seal off potentially hazardous zones or sections where the hole may be unstable.

Production casing is run when the company has decided that the well is capable of production and to isolate the productive zones.

Each string of pipe is cemented inside the preceding string of casing. Cement is pumped down inside a particular piece of casing, circulated around the outside and back up to the surface to create a concrete sheath around that piece of casing. It is important to get good cement jobs between each string of casing, which means there is a complete concrete sheath or sleeve surrounding each level of casing. Various things are done to ensure a good cement job, including using a centralizer to centre the casing in the hole before the cement is pumped down the hole. Because each casing string is set within the preceding, larger-diameter casing string, the diameter of the hole becomes smaller and smaller. The last piece of pipe, the production casing, is commonly only ten centimetres (four inches) in diameter.

While the well is being drilled, a column or string of drill pipe known as the drill string fits inside the casing. The drill string transmits the mud or drilling fluid and power or torque to the drill bit. The term "drill string" often refers to the complete assembly of drill pipe, drill collar, and measurement tools lowered into the hole.

The actual drilling program and the type of casing pipe used depends on a number of factors, including the target depth of the well, the level of groundwater in the area, the formations being drilled through, the contents of the formations, and the pressures that may be encountered. The expected production rates from the well will determine the size of the tubing to be used, which will then impact the type and size of the casing pipe for the various stages of casing. Figure 6 illustrates the various types of casing and tubing string.

Figure 6: Simple cross-section of drill casing

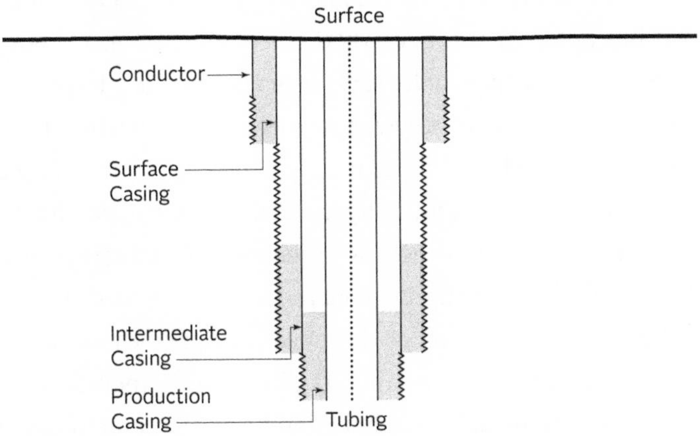

It is always hoped that things go smoothly when drilling, but that is not always the case. Sometimes a foreign object is found in the hole; this is called a fish. A fish could be a chunk of metal (perhaps the result of a lost tool dropped into the hole), a piece of drill bit that has broken off, or a piece of drill string that has separated. The company then has to start a "fishing" operation to try to remove the object so that drilling can continue. Remember that all of this activity, including the drilling, is done within a relatively small-diameter hole (much smaller than the hole you would drill for a fence post). Some of the fishing methods are a magnet to retrieve smaller pieces of iron; a spear, which tries to hold the fish by friction; milling, which grinds away on the pipe to get an effective contact point; and jars to loosen the fish. Many drilling budgets have been overshot due to the need for multiple fishing trips.

Sometimes a well needs to be directionally drilled or "whipstocked" in order for the bottomhole to reach the ultimate formation target. This can be built into the initial drilling program, particularly if the surface location above the target is inaccessible, such as when there is a large lake, river, or roadway. However, sometimes the well needs to be whipstocked while drilling if a large object is encountered that cannot be drilled out by the drill bit. A wedge-shaped device is placed in the hole at a predetermined depth, which causes the drill string to deviate in the desired direction. Directional survey tools are lowered into the hole to measure the deviation and determine its direction. Remember that this might all be done in a hole that has a diameter of ten to twenty-five centimetres (four to ten inches), potentially hundreds or thousands of metres below the surface of the land.

Completions

While the main purpose of drilling a well is to see if hydrocarbons are present in the formation(s) of interest, completing a well determines if the well can be produced economically. Various techniques are applied to the well by completion engineers to see if the formation can be produced at a rate that is economic for the company.

You will recall that there can be a few layers of casing and cement sheaths or sleeves around the various casing strings. Once various formation evaluation techniques are used to identify potential productive zones, the next step is to make small holes through the casing strings over these potentially productive zones to access the formation. These are called perforations, and a perforating gun is used to make them. The perforating gun delivers a small explosive charge to create a hole in the casing and the surrounding rock. The gun is fired electronically from the surface, with multiple shots fired at a time. As with any technology, the design of perforating guns has evolved over time, but the basic principles remain the same. The point is to form carefully placed holes in the casing in order to access the productive formations that sit on the other side.

Once the well has been perforated, hydrochloric acid is often run over the perforations to dissolve and wash away small particles of rock matrix that may be in the perforations. The hope is that this stimulation will then allow the hydrocarbons to flow into the wellbore. This isn't always the case, and a further level of stimulation must be used.

Typically, the next level of stimulation is fracing—short for fracturing. This involves subjecting the formation to high pressures that cause the formation to break or fracture. Materials used to create these high pressures and to frac depend on the makeup (matrix) of the target formation. The material used could be sand, water, or a gas (such as nitrogen). Fracing is a science all on its own.

Once the formation has been fractured, sand is pumped into the fractures to keep them open. In the case of a formation that is already made up of a sand base, adding sand to the fractures keeps the spaces between the grains of sand open, thereby increasing the porosity. In the case of coal or shale, fracing attempts to open or crack the rock and then fill up these cracks with sand to keep them open and provide a conduit for the gas or oil to flow to the wellbore. Think of this as creating highways for the natural gas or oil to flow to the wellbore and ultimately to the surface, where it can be produced and captured.

If the prospect is in an exploratory phase, finding the best material to use when fracing a well is an experimental process. The company that first figures out the appropriate frac substance for a particular formation has an advantage over its competitors for a short period while the other companies determine what works. An example of where different frac substances needed to be tried is the coal in the Western

Canadian Sedimentary Basin. After trying various materials, companies found that water was not a good frac substance, as the targeted Horseshoe Canyon coal was dry (i.e., did not naturally contain water). When water was introduced into the formation, it was then very hard, if not impossible, to get it out. After some experimentation, companies ended up fracing with nitrogen, which was good for a couple of reasons. Nitrogen did not react with the matrix, and it could be pumped into the formation at high pressure, thereby expanding and extending the natural fracture system already in the coals.

Fracing is not a new process; the oil and gas industry has been using it for years to stimulate wells to produce. However, it has moved into the spotlight recently with the advent of unconventional resource plays such as coalbed methane and particularly shale. For the latter, companies are able to pump multiple fracs in the horizontal leg of a wellbore, thus creating more highways in the formation that natural gas and oil can use to travel to the wellbore and then to the surface and ultimately production.

Shale plays have attracted attention primarily due to the size of the fracs (how much frac material is pumped into the formation), the high pressures that are needed to pump in the frac material to make the shale produce, and the tremendous amount of resources, particularly water, that are used in the process. Concerns have also been raised about the chemicals that may be in the frac fluids injected into the formations and the potential risk of groundwater contamination. If you think back to the mechanics of drilling a well, you may recall the concrete sheaths that are built around the various sections of casing. With good cement jobs, the risk of groundwater contamination is low because fracing is typically conducted much deeper than where the groundwater aquifers are located, which means that frac fluids should not come in contact with groundwater sources.

During the completion process or the production testing process, it is sometimes necessary to ignite a well and flare the gas coming out of it. If an oil well also has gas in the formation, a company must produce both the oil and the gas in order to get a read on how much oil the well can produce. The company can always collect (and potentially produce and sell) the oil that comes to the surface, but it is difficult to do that when gas also comes up the wellbore. Typically, the gas is diverted and flared. With a gas well capable of producing gas at high rates, flaring during the production testing phase is often done to get a true indication of how much gas is coming out of that wellbore. Flaring is done under strict rules and regulations monitored by the energy regulator of a particular jurisdiction, and there are usually limits as to how much gas can be flared and over what period.

Equipping, Tie-in, and Pipelining

Once completion operations are finished and the formations are flowing into the wellbore, the well is turned over to production engineers who determine what equipment is necessary to produce the well. The type of equipment required depends on a number of factors, including whether the well is oil or gas, whether it is sweet or sour, the initial rate of production, and how far the well is from infrastructure. Production engineers then arrange for the installation of the required equipment so the well can produce.

A string of pipe known as tubing is installed inside the production casing. The typical diameter of tubing is from five to ten centimetres (two to four inches). The tubing can be left hanging free or it may be held rigid by a production packer that allows a tight seal between the tubing string and the production casing. It is possible to have multiple tubing strings (typically a maximum of four) within the production casing to produce from different formations. Each tubing string would be isolated from the other producing formations through the use of packers. Different sizes of tubing could be used depending on the expected production from the formation. If the tubing is too small, production may be restricted. If the tubing is too large, there will be wasted additional cost for both the actual tubing as well as the various casing strings, which would all need to be larger to accommodate the larger tubing.

Hydrocarbons are typically produced up the tubing, but sometimes, when a company wants to produce another formation, the cost of running another tubing string or the restricted size of the casing may make the company decide to produce both up the tubing string and in the annulus space between the tubing string and the production casing.

If there are pipelines nearby that can take production from the area to a central facility for further processing, a short pipeline might be laid to connect the well to the main gathering system, and the well can be tied in. If there is no pipeline infrastructure nearby and the well is a gas well, it will likely have to be shut in until pipelines are available to bring the gas to market. If there is no nearby infrastructure and the well is an oil well, the oil can be accumulated in tanks on the wellsite and then trucked to a processing facility.

Production Operations

Once the well is on production, the engineer's role does not end. It is the production engineer's job to keep the well producing at optimal levels to ensure that as much resource as possible is extracted from that well. I refer to production at optimal levels rather than maximum levels, since circumstances sometimes dictate that a well be produced at less-than-maximum levels. For example, if an oil reservoir is sitting on top of a water reservoir, you do not want to draw on the oil reservoir too hard by producing it at maximum levels, as that may cause the water to come up and flow into the wellbore. This results in the well watering out; there will likely not be any more oil production from that particular well, and it will have to be abandoned. Think of it as having a straw in the formation and trying to suck up only the top layer. If you suck too hard on the straw, you will draw in the fluid from the lower layers.

Production levels from each well are closely monitored; if there is a drop in production, the production or operations engineers try to figure out the reason and then rectify it to bring the production back up. For example, if the perforations have become slightly plugged over time, washing them with hydrochloric acid (known as an acid job) will re-open them. Sometimes minute amounts of formation water may accumulate in the bottom of the wellbore, thereby affecting relative pressure between the formation and the wellbore. This water needs to be swabbed out of the wellbore to restore the pressure differential so that the formation fluid (or gas) can flow into the wellbore again.

If production levels are decreasing due to something happening in the reservoir, the production engineer works with the geologist to try to determine a cause. They may propose a re-completion of the producing formation to enhance the production rates. If the geologist feels that a particular producing formation is depleted, he may propose that the company move up the hole to attempt a completion on a shallower horizon or formation. If all the formations are depleted and there are no further prospective formations in the wellbore, the operations engineer then prepares to abandon the wellbore, all in accordance with the appropriate regulations.

Once the well is properly abandoned, the company will work to restore the site to its original state. In many jurisdictions, a company is allowed to surrender the surface lease for a site only when the site has been restored and reclaimed. The lease covering the mineral rights may expire before the well is abandoned, but the company must keep up with its obligations under the surface lease until the site has been fully restored and reclaimed, which could take many years. In some jurisdictions, it is necessary to get a reclamation certificate from a regulatory body before the surface lease can be surrendered back to the surface landowner.

Primary, Secondary, and Enhanced Recovery

If a company goes through the steps outlined above to drill and complete a well, it may achieve production from that well and, if it has a number of wells in the vicinity, from that pool or field for a considerable length of time. In many conventional oil and gas prospects, there is enough pressure in the formation to force the hydrocarbons into the well and up the tubing string to the surface. Sometimes there is enough formation pressure to force the hydrocarbon (usually crude oil) into the well, but not enough to push it to the surface. In this case, some form of artificial lift is added to help the crude oil move to the surface. A pump (seen on the surface as the familiar piece of equipment known as a pumpjack) is one form of artificial lift. Another is a gas lift, which is the injection of gas into the crude oil so that the density of the oil decreases and the formation pressure can push it to the surface. Production that depends mainly on reservoir pressure to push the hydrocarbons into the well is known as primary recovery.

When the pressure in the reservoir has decreased to the point where it is no longer able to push the crude oil into the wellbore, companies will look at methods to increase the pressure in the reservoir, particularly if the hydrocarbons are shown to be able to move freely through a reservoir. Typically, this involves injection of either gas or water into the reservoir system. When gas is injected, it is usually put into the top of the reservoir, where it can then push the crude oil into the production tubing. When water is injected, this is known as a waterflood. Water is injected into a few carefully selected wells in an oilfield, and the oil is then pushed toward the remaining producing wells. This assumes that the rock properties will allow these mechanics to work. This also assumes that some contractual arrangement is in place among all of the companies that hold the mineral rights in the pool. Another type of water injection is to inject water into an aquifer in the same reservoir formation. The addition of the water will help to maintain the reservoir pressure. When companies need to increase the pressure in the reservoir through these methods, this is known as secondary recovery. See Figures 7 and 8 for some examples of secondary recovery schemes.

Primary and secondary recovery schemes can still leave a lot of oil in the ground. Companies will then look at other methods to get this remaining oil out of the reservoir. These are often known as tertiary recovery or enhanced recovery schemes.

An example of an enhanced recovery project is when methane gas or petroleum in gas vapour form is injected into the reservoir to mix with the remaining oil. The oil and gas mixture can then be captured at the surface and separated. This is a form of miscible recovery scheme.

Figure 7: Secondary recovery—gas over oil over water

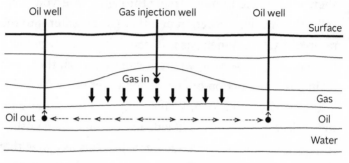

Increased pressure on oil reservoir

Oil migrates to oil well wellbores— areas of lower pressure

Figure 8: Simple waterflood

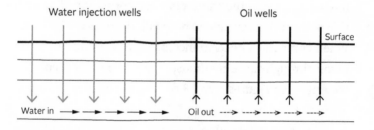

Top view

W	W -->	O	
W -->	O	O	
W	W -->	O	O

W   Water injection well

O   Oil well

-->   Flow of water

Pattern and distance between wells is designed depending on characteristics of reservoir formation.

Another enhanced recovery project may inject hot steam into a reservoir. The idea here is to make the oil less viscous so it can flow into the wellbore and be captured. Think what happens when you heat oil; it flows much more easily. This is a form of thermal recovery scheme.

Still another enhanced recovery project is known as gas cycling. Some natural gas reservoirs contain a large amount of heavier hydrocarbons in a gas state. As the products are brought to the surface, they revert to liquid form due to the decrease in pressure and temperature. This is what is meant when someone says that a well is producing liquids-rich gas. In the reservoir, if the pressure is allowed to decline, some of these heavier hydrocarbons will condense out and the company will not be able to produce them. One way to maintain the pressure is to produce the hydrocarbons, remove the liquids, and re-inject the now dry gas. The company can produce and sell the liquids removed from the gas and eventually produce the dry gas from the reservoir.

As the production decreases from a pool, a company may want to use methods to increase or maintain the recovery from that pool before moving ahead to abandoning the wells. As we have seen in this discussion, there are many different, often ingenious, ways to enhance production. Whether a secondary or an enhanced recovery project is initiated depends primarily on the characteristics of the reservoir, the costs associated with the project, the expected recovery, and how long it will take to capture the additional production. There is no point in initiating a project if the costs exceed the expected additional recovery from the reservoir.

Conventional versus Unconventional Resource Plays

As I indicated in Chapter 1, companies are now drilling into and producing from source rocks and not just reservoir rocks. What follows is a brief summary of how exploring for unconventional resources differs from conventional plays.

MINERAL LAND

Due to the size and extent of an unconventional play, companies want to tie up as much mineral land as possible over the play and have their mineral rights be as geographically contiguous as possible over an extended area. In most cases, the question isn't whether the source rock is present, it's whether the well(s) can be effectively and efficiently drilled and completed. Securing a large, contiguous block of land allows a company to produce from the minimum number of wells necessary to extract the resource.

SURFACE LAND

On resource plays such as coalbed methane, where the target formations are relatively shallow, small wellsites are leased, as these are typically minimal-disturbance locations. Many wellsites (two to sixteen) may be required on a section of land to effectively capture the resource below that section. Because these are gas wells on minimal-disturbance sites with little need for a lot of above-ground equipment, the surface landowner can often continue to farm or otherwise use the land right up to small fenced areas that may each contain some pipes and valves sticking out of the ground. On deeper resource plays such as shale gas and oil, the wellsites are usually larger, because there is likely more than one well being drilled from the drilling padsite.

DRILLING

There is little difference between drilling a shallow unconventional resource play and drilling a shallow gas well. Drilling times tend to be relatively short (a day or two), with few complications. Drilling a deeper shale play is more complicated and will often involve the drilling of horizontal wells. Sometimes a vertical well is drilled first to confirm the depths of the various formations; this is often referred to as a pilot hole. A position is then selected for the placement of a wedge-shaped tool (similar to the ones used in whipstocking a well). Because it is impossible for a drill string to make a ninety-degree angle, a part of the hole—referred to as the build section—allows the drill string to slowly bend. The hope is that the build section has been calculated correctly so that the drill bit can land in the formation and continue drilling horizontally.

I think it is quite amazing that a drill bit can be steered from the surface when it is located many thousands of metres below. As technology advances, longer and longer horizontal wells are being drilled. Horizontal wells started with a horizontal reach of 1,000 metres (3,300 feet), but we are now able to reach horizontal lengths of 2,500 to 3,000 metres (approximately 8,000 to 10,000 feet).

COMPLETIONS

In a shallow unconventional resource play, it is often necessary to frac the formations before they will produce. In the Horseshoe Canyon coalbed methane play in western

Canada, for example, nitrogen is used to frac the coals so that methane gas will flow into the wellbore. In the deeper unconventional resource plays where horizontal wells have been drilled through the formation, multi-stage fracs are done throughout the horizontal leg of the wellbore, thus opening a lot of the rock to the wellbore. Just as the drilling of wells has expanded due to advances in technology, so has the completion part of the puzzle. There have been increases in the number of fracs that can be done at one time, the number of total fracs that can be put into a wellbore, and the extent or reach of those fracs.

EQUIPPING, PIPELINING, AND PRODUCTION

Once drilled, an unconventional shallow gas resource play is often treated like any other shallow gas play. In some instances and reservoirs, there is the need to handle a large volume of water produced with the gas. For deeper shale plays, because there are often multiple wells on a single drilling pad, the production from each of the wells is measured before being collected into a single line to go to a processing facility. As with other wells, production rates are monitored closely in order to maintain the optimal production from each well.

Health and Safety

As you can see, drilling, testing, and completing a well are very complex operations, and there is a lot of potential for accidents. Even when a well is being operated for production, there are many opportunities for things to go wrong. Operations in the oil and gas industry often involve a lot of large equipment, sometimes operating simultaneously, and exposure to a number of chemicals and elements, both manmade and natural. Safety is paramount to any operator's activities.

Most companies have at least one individual responsible for health and safety issues, whether they are an employee or a consultant. Before any field operation, a safety meeting is usually held to ensure that all personnel are aware of and understand the processes and risks involved. Most, if not all, companies adhere to safety standards. Often, these safety standards have been developed by industry organizations and are adopted by all companies working in the industry. Companies take the health and safety of their employees and contractors seriously, as their human resources are critical to their success in this highly competitive industry.

Key Points in This Chapter

- Drilling and completing an oil and gas well is a complex process and involves many different skill sets.

- The type of rig required to drill a well will depend on the depth of the well, the type of well to be drilled (vertical, directional, horizontal), and the anticipated characteristics of the target formation.

- The drilling program developed by the drilling engineer will consider a number of factors, including whether the well being drilled is an exploratory well or a development well, the type of hydrocarbon expected, the anticipated formation pressures, and the tools required to get the necessary information to evaluate the formation(s).

- Completing a well determines whether the well is commercially viable. Different techniques are used, including perforating, acidizing, and fracing.

- Fracing is not a new technique; the oil and gas industry has used it for many years. It has gained more attention in recent years due to the explosion of drilling activity in shale, which has greatly increased the supply of hydrocarbons, both oil and natural gas. These shale wells require very large fracs to access the hydrocarbons contained in the shale.

- For some reservoirs, enhanced recovery schemes can increase production.

- Many of the steps in the drilling, completion, and production phases need to be modified slightly when exploring for unconventional resources.

- Health and safety issues are important in the oil and gas industry, especially in the operations side of the upstream business.

4

Engineers' World: Evaluations

OFTEN, ENGINEERS ARE involved in evaluating prospects and trying to put a value on them. These engineers
are commonly known as reservoir engineers. This evaluation
process can happen before land is ever acquired on a geologist's play concept, or it can happen after wells have been
drilled. If an evaluation or economics are run on a project
before land is acquired, the company may be trying to decide
whether the expected prize at the end of exploration is worth
the costs and risks involved in entering that play.

Companies also have many choices as to where they
spend their capital. Running economics (i.e., performing
some economic analysis) before entering a play will help a
company decide which plays it should be involved in and how
it should enter the plays. If a company decides to explore for
certain hydrocarbons in a formation, there are many ways it
can potentially enter the prospect. It can acquire the mineral

rights (if they are available) and drill wells on the land, or it can buy existing production and undeveloped land from an operator that is already there. It can choose to pursue this opportunity itself at a 100 percent interest, or it can find a partner to help in a joint venture. Running economics on the various alternatives will help a company make the right choice.

Running Economics to Make Investment Choices

Before a company commits to drilling a well, its engineers usually run economics on the prospect to determine if it is economically viable. A company with a number of prospects will also run economics to rank the opportunities according to some standard parameters and then choose the projects that maximize value for its shareholders. Economic analysis can help a company decide if it should do a project, when it should do it, and how it should be done.

For example, a company can compare the economics of drilling a prospect (new or old) against purchasing production from another company in the same prospect or in a completely different prospect. A good economic model will help the company compare and rank the options against a benchmark to see how much each option will exceed it. Besides projecting a project's cash flow, a good economic model will take into consideration the time value of money— the concept that a dollar today is worth more than a dollar in the future. It will also help a company quantify the risks associated with the project.

It is easy to see how, by using standard parameters, a company can compare different projects to determine which one it should undertake if its investment capital is limited. Of course, if a company is in the enviable position of having unlimited capital, it could do all of the projects that meet or exceed its benchmark. However, the ranking of projects may indicate which projects to do first. The economic model should be easy to apply and provide results that are easily understood by both management and staff.

Here are some common economic models that may be used for simple investment decisions. You may be familiar with some or all of them, perhaps because you have used them in your own personal investment decisions.

PAYBACK MODEL

This model looks at how much time passes before the initial investment is paid back. Generally, a shorter payback time is better than a longer payback time.

PROS:

- Easy to calculate
- People are familiar with the model
- Provides a rough measure of risk, as the longer a project takes, the higher the risk (assuming that the risk of a project is linked to how much time passes before the initial investment is paid back)

CONS:

- Does not take into account the fact that a dollar today is worth more than a dollar in the future (sometimes referred to as the time value of money)

- Does not take into account the cash flow that may come in after payback has occurred
- Does not put a number to the risk; it only roughly measures it

RETURN ON INVESTMENT MODEL

Broadly speaking, this model looks at the annual profit of a project divided by the value of the investment (in accounting terms, the remaining book value). Generally, a higher return on investment is better than a lower one.

PROS:

- Easy to calculate
- Uses terms and concepts familiar to accountants and financial people

CONS:

- Does not take into account the time value of money
- Book value and profit do not always match the actual cash in and out on the project
- Book value of the investment is not always equal to the actual salvage or market value of the investment

COST-BENEFIT RATIO MODEL

This is a simple calculation of dividing the costs of a project by its benefits, usually all measured in dollars. The lower the ratio, the better the project.

PROS:

- Easy to calculate
- Possible to include and consider an approximate cost or benefit that is not strictly cash; for example, if there is the

potential to do a similar deal to the one currently being considered, what is the approximate incremental value of that future deal to the company?

CONS:

- Does not consider the time value of money
- Need to be careful when trying to place a value on an intangible cost or benefit, such as a company's reputation and its ability to continue to work in an area

DISCOUNTED CASH FLOWS AND NET PRESENT VALUES

In each of the three models discussed thus far, a missing component is the time value of money, which is an important concept to include when looking at large, complex projects. Simply stated, this assumes that a dollar that you have today is worth more than a dollar in the future, because the dollar you have today has the potential to earn interest. Granted, in a low-interest environment, the interest you earn on a single dollar may not be very much. However, when that interest is applied to hundreds or thousands or millions of dollars, it can add up to a significant amount.

The exercise, then, is to figure out what the future cash flows from a project are worth today. This is done by taking the total of future cash flows from the project and dividing it by one plus a discount rate, which is an approximation of the interest rate that you could get if you were to simply invest the money with, for example, a bank. This comparison assumes that the risk is the same between various choices, which may not always be an accurate assumption.

When you build in the amount and timing of costs associated with a project and the amount and timing of cash flows expected from the project, and then apply the concept of the time value of money, you can discount both costs and cash flows to what they are worth today. You can then determine what is known as the net present value (NPV) of the project today.

The NPVs of different projects can be calculated and ranked to help a company decide which projects they should proceed with. While this is the primary economic model used in the oil and gas industry, other tools, such as the ones discussed earlier, can also be used in the decision-making process. For example, if two projects have similar NPVs but one project has a substantially quicker payback, the project with the quicker payback may be the best project to choose.

Compared to the other models, calculating NPV to evaluate projects is more complex (although computer models have been built to do the calculations), and the model is a little more difficult to understand (it's not likely that you or I will choose this method to evaluate our personal investment decisions). However, when companies are evaluating projects that are very expensive and will be in existence for many, many years, it is a very valuable tool in deciding which project will add the most value for the shareholders.

Calculating Reserves

Once a well or wells have been drilled in a play, the reservoir engineer will also be asked to evaluate the worth of the

resources that have been found. They do this by trying to estimate the production expected from the wells drilled to date
over the life of each well. They also may project the reserves
over the entire prospect by building a model of a development plan that shows when additional wells will be drilled
into a play and the expected production from those wells.
The geologists may also be asked to provide information
about the extent of the play, both vertically and horizontally.

There is a distinction between the resource potential of
a play and the recoverable reserves. An estimated recovery
factor is applied to the resource potential to predict how
much of the resource can actually be recovered and produced out of the ground. Reserves are the amount that can
be commercially produced from a given point in time.

All reserve numbers have some amount of uncertainty.
The degree of uncertainty depends on how much data is
available, both geological and engineering. The reservoir
engineers develop some of their reserves information using
a type curve, which is a profile of the expected production
out of a well over the time that the well will be producing.
On resource plays, they develop a type curve for a formation
using the performance information they have to date from
existing wells and production. A type curve for a formation
shows the expected production from a new well drilled into
the play, and it is a benchmark that new wells are measured
against. If many of the wells drilled on the prospect do not
fall along the type curves, the type curves may need to be
re-examined and adjusted.

Reserves are reported in volumes. Companies typically
adhere to standard definitions for different classifications of

reserves. Both the Society of Petroleum Engineers (SPE) and the World Petroleum Council (WPC) provide standards in an attempt to achieve more consistent reporting of reserves, particularly with unproved reserves. The main reserve categories are proved reserves and unproved reserves, with unproved reserves being more uncertain.

Proved reserves are the estimated volume of hydrocarbons that a company believes with reasonable certainty it can produce at a profit. Generally, proved reserves depend on actual production or direct tests on a formation. Proved reserves can be further classified as developed or undeveloped. Proved developed reserves are already producing. If proved reserves are classified as undeveloped (i.e., not yet producing), it is likely because the well logs and/or core data from the non-producing well show reservoirs that are similar to producing wells in the area or formation evaluation tests show they can be produced. Reservoir engineers also apply other criteria to classify reserves as proved.

Unproved reserves are also based on geologic and engineering data, but there are too many uncertainties—whether technical, economic, contractual, and/or regulatory—to allow the hydrocarbons to be classified as proved. Unproved reserves can be further divided into probable reserves and possible reserves, with possible reserves having the greater uncertainty.

To be classified as probable, there has to be a better chance of recovering the unproved reserves than not. The SPE and WPC have suggested a number of situations that would qualify unproved reserves as probable.

Possible unproved reserves are less likely to be recovered for various reasons. Again, there are a number of scenarios where unproved reserves would qualify as possible reserves.

Adding the component of price forecasts over time, the expected future cash flows from the existing well(s) and any well(s) drilled in the future can be calculated. The value of the reserves in today's dollars can be calculated by applying a discount rate to the future cash flows.

Looking at the recoverable reserves over the entire play, an engineer can also estimate the costs to drill the entire play and the timing of additional drilling. Applying an appropriate discount rate to the future costs will bring the costs back to present-day dollars. With the present-day costs and the present-day value of the recoverable reserves, the NPV for the prospect can be calculated.

Many variables can affect the reserves calculation. For example, the type curve that is used will impact the volume of reserves calculated. Whether the price forecast is optimistic or pessimistic will also affect the NPV of those reserves.

Even if you are not interested in reserves from an operational perspective, this discussion about reserves is important if you are an investor in oil and gas stocks, as companies are required to disclose or file their reserves under their particular listing jurisdiction. A company's bank may also want to see what the reserves of the company look like over time.

Key Points in This Chapter

- Economic evaluations can be applied on a project to see if it is worthwhile to pursue and how it ranks against other projects.

- Different types of economic models can be applied to evaluate and compare projects. While a number of simple models can be used, the most valuable models when considering oil and gas projects are those that take into account the time value of money.

- Once a prospect has been drilled, reserves can be calculated for the project. Various factors go into the calculation of reserves, and the reliability of the ultimate results will depend on whether the most appropriate factors have been applied and on the skill of the evaluator.

- Reserves can be classified as proved and unproved. Another level of classification indicates whether the proved reserves are developed or undeveloped and whether the unproved reserves are probable or possible.

- Besides oil and gas companies, other parties who may be interested in estimated reserves are investors (individual and institutional) and the companies' banks.

5

Social Licence to Operate

MUCH HAS BEEN written recently about the need for companies to have a social licence to operate. In fact, a social licence is becoming one of the key elements of managing environmental and social risks. Having a social licence to operate generally means that the local (and sometimes broader) community accepts a company's project or presence in the community. It is quite often intangible and, therefore, difficult to measure, but a company sure knows when it doesn't have its social licence. What does this mean for a company in terms of its planning activities and operations?

Obviously, at a minimum, a company has to abide by the rules, laws, and regulations that apply to their operations. Each jurisdiction has rules and regulations that govern, to name a few, mineral and surface rights, drilling and completion operations, pipelining work, environmental protection, health and safety, and the licensing of the people doing the work. There can be severe penalties and fines for companies that do not abide by the rules and regulations.

While these rules can sometimes be cumbersome, I believe they are good for the industry, as they provide a level playing field for all participants, whether large multinationals or small local operators. Regulations that are monitored, particularly for health, safety, and environmental issues, provide a safe working environment for all involved in the industry and protect the environment so that everyone can continue to enjoy it. However, simply meeting regulatory requirements does not necessarily mean that a company has a social licence to operate.

The process of acquiring a social licence involves developing relationships with the community, Aboriginal and First Nations groups, and other interested parties. The process needs to start early, likely even before a company begins planning the technical aspects of a project. It is critical for a company to be honest and provide accurate information. With social media becoming a much bigger factor in people's consumption of information, news that a company is not honest or provides false information will spread quickly. Good communication skills are necessary, the most important one being active listening. Understanding what values and issues are important to the various groups and finding ways to address the issues is a good way to build a foundation for social licence.

Many large and intermediate-sized companies have a community relations group that manages the relationship between the company and the people in the communities in which it operates. This is particularly important in areas where a company is the major operator or has plans for a major project. In addition to representing their specific firm, the company's personnel are representing the oil and gas industry in the area. If a community's interactions with that company are positive, they will probably have a better perception of the industry in general.

Community relations are especially important when a company is operating an unconventional resource play in the area, such as coalbed methane. These wells are projected to produce over a very long period of time (potentially up to forty or fifty years). Companies operating coalbed methane wells are going to be in the related communities for a very long time; they had better make an effort to be good neighbours. It is common for companies to sponsor local sporting or community activities. Sometimes they even sponsor something tangible with much longer-lasting effects for the community, such as the construction of a health and wellness facility to serve community members.

I believe that the area of stakeholder relations extends beyond community relations to include individuals or groups who do not live directly in the community impacted by the operations. For example, people who live in neighbouring communities could be concerned about increased traffic due to a company's operation. Stakeholders could also include environmental groups that have a particular global cause that a project relates to, or Aboriginal groups who use the area for traditional activities of hunting, fishing, or trapping or who have a historic interest in the area.

Investor relations is another area that could be important in developing the social licence to operate, especially for companies listed on a public stock exchange, although some private companies may also assign an individual to this task. While investors may not necessarily be directly impacted by activities in a certain area, they are concerned about the company's reputation and how that impacts the stock price or perceived value of the company.

Whether it is community, stakeholder, or investor relations, communication is key to developing a social licence—and it is not just about communicating the science, the facts and figures. It is listening to people's concerns, understanding their values, and then having the emotional intelligence to deal with them appropriately.

It has been said that the majority of the technical people in the industry—being primarily engineers and scientists—are not the best communicators. Many in the industry believe that if you just give people the scientific information and facts, they will be convinced that the industry is right. However, science and facts are not the key factors in developing social licence. Many of the issues that stakeholders are currently bringing up produce an emotional response; a scientific explanation will usually not assuage these feelings.

The suggestion then to these companies is to bring people onto the team who have the communication skills needed to address some of these new concerns. These individuals could be external, or they may be internal. Too often, I have seen situations where employees have been categorized into silos on the assumption that they have only those skills directly applicable to their particular profession. Companies would be better off finding out where social licence-building skill sets are already present in the company and engaging those existing employees in this effort.

The increasing importance of having a social licence to operate will also likely impact the way that a company thinks about a project in the planning stages. It will likely need to consider more and more the potential impact on stakeholders beyond the immediate community. By anticipating the issues that may arise, the company can build a certain amount of time into its planning process to address those potential issues.

How we look at the concept of a social licence to operate will need to be broadened as we begin to look at energy from a global perspective. Being granted a social licence to operate goes beyond what an individual company can do. It is my belief that all companies have a responsibility to operate in an honest manner, provide the information people are requesting, and communicate effectively so that the entire industry has a social licence to operate. This is critical to major projects such as a large oil or natural gas pipeline or a proposed large facility.

In a large industry with many diverse players, this can be difficult to achieve. Regulators do their part, and the majority of industry participants do play by the rules and regulations. However, one bad apple can spoil it for the rest of the players in the industry, as that bad example is the one that will hit the press and be circulated through social media. All players in the industry, not just the regulators, have a responsibility to ensure that the industry has a social licence to operate.

Key Points in This Chapter

- Having a social licence to operate is becoming more and more important to companies and the oil and gas industry in general.

- Social licence generally means the acceptance of a project or a company's presence in a community, and it is often intangible and difficult to measure.

- Whether regarding community relations, stakeholder relations, investor relations, or a combination of all three, communication skills are key to developing a company's social licence to operate.

- The most important communication skill is active listening so companies can cultivate relationships with stakeholder groups and understand their values and the issues they raise.

- How we look at social licence to operate will need to be broadened as we start to look at energy from a global perspective.

- Social licence to operate does not apply only to individual companies, but also to the oil and gas industry as a whole.

6

Future Issues

OVER THE PAST few years, many issues have arisen that
have changed the upstream part of the business, and I'm
sure many more developments will arise in the years to come.
In this chapter, I'd like to address some of these current and
emerging issues.

Unconventional Resources

The emergence of unconventional resources has changed the
oil and gas industry in many ways. While some companies
still focus on conventional plays, many others are starting to
focus on unconventional resource plays where they can drill
into the source rocks. Even though the costs to drill and complete these wells is very high compared to conventional plays,
these wells typically produce, on average, at much higher
rates than wells drilled into conventional reservoirs.

Besides changing the targets that companies are going after and how the wells are drilled and completed, the large volumes being produced from unconventional resources are also changing the supply and demand picture in North America and globally. Rising oil prices in the early 2000s due to increased global demand encouraged companies to look at new ways to drill and complete formerly difficult reservoirs. By the middle of the 2000s, North American supply of oil and gas rose significantly as a result of improved extraction technologies. However, global supply remained about the same due to political conflicts in other oil-producing regions of the world that restricted their supply to the global market.

As American companies have had a lot of success drilling unconventional natural gas resources, particularly from shale gas plays, they are not importing as much natural gas from Canada. Companies drilling in Canada are also having tremendous success in drilling unconventional shale gas resources and are trying to find other markets for the natural gas they are producing. This is what is currently driving the discussions about exporting liquefied natural gas (LNG) from the west coast of Canada to markets in Asia.

The success in the United States of drilling for shale oil, combined with other factors in the global supply picture, has driven the price of oil downward as of the writing of this book. The increase in supply coming from North America has also caught the attention of the Organization of the Petroleum Exporting Countries (OPEC) as it looks to address its global market share in the face of declining oil prices.

While lower oil prices may be good for drivers as the price at the gas pump falls to reflect the lower price for a barrel of oil, there are other ramifications. Provinces, states, or countries that rely on royalties from the production of oil and gas on government-owned lands may need to start revising budgets to reflect a decrease in their revenues. Decreased revenues could mean a reduction in the services or infrastructure that governments provide their constituents.

If oil prices remain low for an extended period of time, companies may reduce their drilling activities substantially, as some of the higher-cost projects may no longer be economic. This could result in reduced staff levels, which could then impact the local economy, particularly if it is heavily focused and dependent on the oil and gas sector. Consumer consumption could decrease because people will have fewer dollars to spend on items. Falling oil prices could cause many local economic impacts that may not be initially obvious. Even people who are not directly employed by an oil and gas company will be affected as impacts trickle through the economy.

Transportation of Products

The success in drilling unconventional resources has led to an increased supply of hydrocarbons in the North American market. While this is significant, most of us will not see any tangible benefit from this increase if the product cannot get to market.

There are many different types of pipelines. There are those that carry different liquid petroleum products from the field to refineries and then from refineries to end users or export facilities. Gas gathering pipelines take gas from individual wells to gas processing plants. Gas transmission pipelines then take gas from processing plants to distribution centres. From the distribution centres, gas distribution pipelines carry natural gas to the ultimate end users, whether businesses or residences. There is a network of millions of kilometres of pipelines throughout Canada and the United States. However, many of these pipelines are at capacity, and some sections need to be replaced due to age.

A couple of key pipelines that have been in the news recently are the Keystone XL pipeline project and the Northern Gateway pipeline project. Keystone XL is designed to transport crude oil from fields in western Canada down to refineries in the Gulf Coast area of the United States, where the crude oil will be processed into a number of refined products. Northern Gateway is designed to transport crude oil from Alberta oilfields through British Columbia for eventual export to Pacific Rim nations. I do not plan to debate the pros and cons of these pipeline projects in this book, as there are many issues to be considered for each pipeline. I do hope, however, that with the background information contained in this book, you will feel more comfortable conducting your own research and come to your own conclusions.

Pipelines are not the only way to get the product to market. Liquid hydrocarbons can also be transported around North America by truck or rail. Once liquid hydrocarbons arrive at a port, they can be loaded onto a ship or oil tanker and sail to their market destination, where they will be off-loaded and then transported to ultimate end users by truck, rail, or pipeline, depending on the infrastructure present in that market.

Similarly, once natural gas can get to a port, it can be liquefied through a process involving extreme cooling of the gas and then be transported by a ship or LNG tanker to a port near its ultimate market. When it arrives, it will need to go through a regas facility to turn it back into gas before it is sent, likely by pipeline, to its ultimate end users.

The key in each of these scenarios is that the petroleum product has to get to its market via some form of transportation. The costs and benefits of each mode of transport need to be considered, as do the risks involved with each method. Safety is a key consideration both in terms of the workers who must handle the product as well as the communities that the product passes through.

Supply and Demand: Global Market

As briefly discussed above, the success we have had in North America is impacting the supply and demand of petroleum products on a global basis. Sometimes whether a particular facility is an import or export facility depends on the location of the supply and on the infrastructure in the region. Does the infrastructure exist to take a supply out of the region, or is it easier to export it to a willing buyer at a nearby facility?

The following is an example of how the supply and demand dynamics have shifted in North America. Canada has vast energy resources and has traditionally looked to the United States as its main export market. However, due to the success that companies have had drilling unconventional resources in the United States, Canada can no longer depend on the country as a primary customer for its petroleum products. Canadian companies are looking for other customers outside of North America. Asia has emerged as a major potential customer, since many Asian countries are looking for reliable sources of oil and gas to fuel their growing economies.

As of the writing of this book, there are some major logistics that have to be overcome before exports to Asia can occur. There is, of course, the huge ocean separating Canada from Asia. There also needs to be at least one, and likely more than one, major LNG terminal built on the west coast of Canada that will, at minimum, consist of facilities to cool and thus liquefy the natural gas and a deep water port. Pipelines need to be built or expanded to transport natural gas from the wells to the export facility.

While this discussion focuses on natural gas, the Northern Gateway pipeline project mentioned earlier proposes to transport crude oil from the oilfields of Alberta to an export facility. Wells need to be drilled to ensure a reliable, long-term supply to these markets. A large workforce is also required for many pieces of this puzzle.

Besides the logistics, government policies are needed so that companies considering the investment of billions of dollars know the framework within which they will be operating. While all of this is going on in Canada, it is critical to understand that we operate within a global energy economy.

Other countries are also pursuing exports through LNG terminals and export facilities. Some of these LNG terminals are already operating and potentially undergoing expansion, while others are still under construction. Countries such as the United States, Australia, and Qatar are Canada's competitors in the race to provide LNG facilities.

Considering the complexities of negotiating agreements, building an LNG facility, and developing government policies, it seems like a very daunting task. However, given the ingenuity of Canadians, their ability to see the bigger picture, and their willingness to work together for larger goals, I am hopeful that Canada will become an exporter of petroleum products on a global scale.

Importance of Stakeholder Involvement and Social Media

As noted in the previous chapter on social licence to operate, stakeholder involvement is very important to the success and progress of the industry. Whether a company is involved at a local level or chooses to play on a global scale, managing the expectations of and working with affected stakeholders is critical. Effective engagement of stakeholders may require many different skill sets within the company.

The explosion in the use of social media makes it critical that companies do the right thing. Why is it that when a company has a misstep, it soars through the Internet, but when it does something right, it's often very quiet? For example, pictures of birds caught in a pond that contains effluent from a processing facility would likely hit the Internet quickly, while a company that provides human resources and materials to help schoolchildren build birdhouses for a wildlife sanctuary will likely not get the same media coverage. It is just as important to celebrate through social media the times when companies do the right thing. Perhaps if companies understood this, there would be more positive stories online.

Competition

The composition of companies within the oil and gas industry has changed, and this is partly due to the large unconventional resource prospects that companies are now pursuing. When I started in the industry over thirty-six years ago, it was common to see an entrepreneur (often a geologist or engineer) raise an amount of money to start a junior oil and gas company. Because the amount of money raised was usually in the $5 to $10 million range, friends and family were often part of the original investor group. The money was likely spent drilling a number of wells on a few different prospects, and once a sufficient amount of production was attained, the prospect or company was sold to an intermediate-sized company. Often, the entrepreneur would take the proceeds and, with the same core group of investors, start the process again.

While some start-up companies may still be trying to do this, the scale they have to do this at is about tenfold, particularly if they are planning to chase unconventional resources. When you consider that drilling one horizontal well into an unconventional resource play could be in the $5 to $7 million range and completing that well could cost another $4 or $5 million, an entrepreneur has to raise significantly more money to start a company today than in the past. Some colleagues in the industry have told me that a more reasonable number to start a company is in the $50 to $100 million range if the company wants to pursue unconventional resources.

If a company wants to pursue more conventional resources, it still can, but the investment required is still significantly more than it was even a few years ago. There are still some individuals who are quite content to operate a few wells in a small geographical area. By keeping an eye on and optimizing the production from the wells, they earn enough money to make a decent living from the operations. People sometimes refer to these as the "mom and pop" operations of the oil and gas industry.

While there are still a few smaller operators in the industry, there has definitely been some consolidation; what we mainly have now in the energy industry are a number of intermediate-sized companies and some very large multinational companies. Part of this is due to the amount of capital needed for large infrastructure projects, particularly if a company wishes to participate in the global energy market. A larger corporation is required in order to attract the investment capital needed to fund large projects. In addition, operating on a global level requires many different skill sets.

While it is possible to contract out some of the tasks, it is desirable to keep many of the key skills within the company.

There is competition not only for financing within the oil and gas industry, but also for human resources. Fewer people have had experience in dealing with unconventional resources. The geology is different, the land deals are slightly different as more land is required, and the drilling and completion of wells are different. While some of our technical professionals are learning and adapting, not all of them are there yet.

A shift in mindset is not always easy for someone who has been in the oil and gas business for many years. It's not quite as extreme as Charles Darwin noted many years ago, "evolve or die," as many veterans in the oil and gas industry may choose to continue to play in the conventional sandbox until they retire. However, those who want to continue working in the industry for a longer period will need to gain some new skills to bolster their experience, and they will need to look at the opportunities in a new light.

As noted earlier in this chapter, we are moving into a global energy economy. There are many ways and places where one can choose to participate in this energy economy. One can choose to participate at a local level with a small operator or as an entrepreneur, or on a global level with a large multinational firm. That is the beauty of our industry: it gives one the flexibility to choose where they wish to contribute.

Multigenerational Workplace and Workforce

Much has been written in the media about the aging of the workforce and the need for more workers to replenish the workforce in light of the number of people expected to retire in the next few years. This is particularly true in the oil and gas industry. There was a period in the early to mid-1980s when hiring more or less came to a standstill in the oil and gas industry, as we were in a down cycle; prices were low and it was difficult to get people to invest in oil and gas. Students did not enter oil and gas–related fields, as the future looked bleak. This created a gap in the industry workforce; we have some veterans with thirty-plus years of experience and we have people with fewer than fifteen or twenty years of experience, with not a lot in between.

We need to find ways to encourage the veterans to stay a little longer in the industry so they can pass on the information they have to the younger group. This works if the veterans are willing to mentor the younger professionals. This does not work if the veterans are either not willing to be mentors or have difficulty doing so because they have not stayed current within their profession.

New entrants to the oil and gas workforce will have new opportunities throughout their careers that may not have been available to previous generations. It's not because the opportunities were not offered to previous generations; it may be because the jobs did not exist within the industry at that time. For example, the rise in the power of computing capacity has led to a dramatic expansion in the modelling programs being used in geology, geophysics, and engineering. Another example comes from the increased importance of a social licence to operate. Professions will likely develop to address these new needs. Looking at issues from a global or generic perspective rather than from the silos of their respective professions will add value. The energy industry and its leaders have to remain open and be willing to look at all issues, not just technical ones, in a creative manner.

The wide age range in the workforce can create some interesting group dynamics, as the work habits, work ethic, and expectations of the different age groups can be very different. If companies want to be successful, they need to ensure that the leaders within their companies have a variety of tools to draw from to effectively manage and motivate their teams. These leaders will need to expand and continually update their skills to manage all the people within their groups. Not everyone is motivated by the same thing, and company leaders must recognize this and adapt accordingly.

Other Sources of Energy

This book is focused on energy from hydrocarbons, but I believe it is worthwhile to mention some of the other main sources of energy, as some are very important in different parts of Canada and the rest of the world.

Hydropower is very important to the generation of electricity in certain parts of Canada, particularly Quebec, Manitoba, British Columbia, Newfoundland and Labrador, and the Yukon. The power of the water drives large turbines that create the needed energy. Sometimes hydropower requires the diversion of water flows and damming in order to create the volume of water necessary to provide the power. In 2013, the US Department of Energy initiated a study of the United States' hydropower assets with the intention of developing a "Hydropower Vision" for their nation. Many other countries such as China, Brazil, Venezuela, Russia, Pakistan, India, and Mexico, to name a few, also have large hydropower facilities.

Solar power is used in various parts of Canada. This appears to be a very attractive option, as sunlight is free, but the upfront costs of a solar power system have been very high. Costs have been dropping for solar units, and some people are leasing portions of solar power systems to make it more affordable. Further, batteries are needed to store some of the energy produced for times when it is stormy or cloudy and for nighttime electricity use. Considerations when one is thinking about solar power are location, the costs to produce the panels and cells, the efficiency and reliability of the power system, and the area required to install a system. Large solar power plants and facilities are located in China, Spain, Germany, France, Portugal, India, and the United States.

Wind power is used to some extent in every province in Canada, with Alberta, Ontario, and Quebec the leaders. While seen as a renewable source of energy, wind power is also a way to diversify the energy supply from other sources such as fossil fuels and hydropower. Large areas are required for the installation of wind turbines. Wind farms are located throughout the world, including in the United States (particularly in California, Texas, Oregon, and Colorado, to name a few states), the United Kingdom, China, and Australia.

Nuclear power is also used to create electricity in Canada, primarily in Ontario and in one plant in New Brunswick. Current public sentiment about nuclear facilities is not very positive. Negative opinions tend to rise when an incident or accident occurs at a nuclear facility. Countries such as France, Japan, Russia, South Korea, China, India, and the United States have a large number of nuclear power plants in operation.

Gas hydrates are solids that have a crystalline form. Essentially, gas molecules are captured by water molecules in a solid form. When you think of water in a solid form, you probably think of ice. However, in this case, because gas molecules are captured within the solid water, this solid will burn. It has been determined that there are large quantities of gas hydrates deep in the ocean off the west coast of Canada. However, at the time of the writing of this book, we do not have an economic method of recovering these gas hydrates.

In my opinion, none of the other energy sources described above are able to completely replace hydrocarbons as a primary source of energy at this time. Each of these other sources of energy requires investment in further infrastructure and/or research before any can become dominant. It is likely that we will see a blend of energy sources being used for many years to come, with the particular blend in any given area dependent on the characteristics of the region and the types of energy that can be produced efficiently and cost-effectively there.

Key Points in This Chapter

- Companies have been very successful in advancing the technologies required to produce oil and gas from unconventional resources such that they are now producing oil and gas from rocks such as shale, coal, and tight sand.

- The success that companies have had in drilling for unconventional resources has changed the exploration process and how we look at geology, land acquisition, drilling, and completions.

- Since we now have many more resources to produce, we need to look at ways to expand the transportation system.

- The emergence of unconventional resources has shifted the supply and demand picture in North America.

- Canada can no longer view the United States as its major customer for petroleum products; it is now looking at new markets such as Asia.

- Increased production of oil and natural gas from the United States has had an impact on the global supply.

- Many steps need to be taken in order for Canada to participate in the global LNG market, such as the creation of a government policy framework, the building or expansion of pipelines, the development of a workforce, and the development of an LNG terminal.

- The explosion of social media makes stakeholder engagement even more important for the oil and gas industry.

- The size and structure of start-up companies in the oil and gas sector have changed due to the need for more capital to pursue exploration.

- The energy industry and its leaders must look at all issues, technical and non-technical, in a creative manner.

- Multigenerational workforces require company leaders to evolve so they can motivate and manage expectations of their employees differently.

- Other sources of energy are being used to generate electricity, but it is unlikely that any one of these sources can currently replace hydrocarbons. A blend of energy sources will likely be used for the foreseeable future.

7

Final Thoughts
―――――――――――――

Tᴴɪѕ ʙᴏᴏᴋ ɪѕ intended to provide the average person on
the street with a base of knowledge about the upstream
side of the oil and gas industry. Using simple language and
concepts, I have attempted to describe how oil and gas are
formed, how they are found, and how we get them out of the
ground.

With this basic knowledge, I hope you are more comfortable thinking about issues such as pipelines and
transportation to take the oil and gas found in Canada to
where the markets are, even if the markets are halfway
around the world. I also hope the information contained in
this book gives you a starting point from which to ask questions of the people spouting various opinions about the
oil and gas industry. If you have a knowledge base to start
from, you are in a much better position to ask questions, for-
mulate your own opinions, and make your own decisions

surrounding the future of energy in your life. At the back of this book, I have identified some other resources where you can find further information to continue learning about the oil and gas industry.

Energy is an important topic, as it affects each of us on a daily basis. If you are interested in joining the discussions surrounding energy, I challenge you to educate yourself so that you are better equipped to understand the discussion points and reach your own conclusions. Since energy affects each one of us as well as future generations, I encourage you to become involved in the conversation.

If after reading this book you have a better understanding about the oil and gas industry and feel more comfortable engaging in the conversation about energy, then I have accomplished my main goal.

Sources of Further Information

Alberta Energy (www.energy.gov.ab.ca)

This is the Government of Alberta department that deals with Crown lands. Here you can find information not only on Crown ownership of lands but also about the various resources in the province, energy legislation, maps, and the calculation of royalties on Crown lands.

Alberta Energy Regulator (www.aer.ca)

The Alberta Energy Regulator regulates oil and gas activity in the province. Besides outlining the process that companies need to go through, the website provides data about daily drilling activity, a map of abandoned wells, rules and directives that a company must follow, decisions of hearings, and advice on how to get involved in the exploration and production process, among other items.

Canadian Association of Petroleum Producers (www.capp.ca)

This is an industry-based organization for Canada's oil and natural gas producers whose website contains a lot of information that anyone interested in the oil and gas industry would find educational. Under the Library & Statistics tab is a Publications section that provides information on a variety of subjects. Under the Statistics section is a good historical summary of the petroleum industry in Canada called the *Statistical Handbook*.

Canadian Society for Unconventional Resources (www.csur.com)

As its name implies, this association supports the exploration and development of unconventional resources in Canada. Its website has a strong emphasis on the transfer of technical information among different groups. Under the Resources tab are fact sheets, booklets, presentations, and videos about these developing resources.

Pembina Institute (www.pembina.org)

This organization focuses on protecting Canada's environment by advancing clean energy solutions. Under the Publications tab are numerous publications addressing various energy issues and their impacts on the environment and the economy.

Frequently Used Terms

About the Author

LEVONNE LOUIE IS an oil and gas professional with over thirty-six years of experience in negotiations, government relations, business development, strategy development, mediation, and coaching. She has a Master of Business Administration, a Bachelor of Commerce, and a Bachelor of Science, all from the University of Calgary. She has been a member of the Canadian Association of Petroleum Land-men (CAPL) since 1980; she was granted the Professional Landman designation in 1990, and she served three terms on the board of CAPL. A graduate of the Directors Education Program of the Institute of Corporate Directors, Ms. Louie was granted the ICD.D designation in 2011. She currently serves as a board member of Alberta Theatre Projects and the Calgary Convention Centre Authority.

CPSIA information can be obtained
at www.ICGtesting.com
Printed in the USA
BVHW04s1737040518
515196BV00002BA/134/P